Tones That Are Tender
Percy French
1854 – 1920

Berrie O'Neill was born in 1930 on a farm near Eyrecourt, County Galway. He enjoyed a long career with the Bank of Ireland in Dublin and Belfast during which time he served a term as president of the Irish Association for Cultural, Economic and Social relations. He is now president of the Percy French Society in North Down, and lives in Belfast with his wife Gladys.

To Gladys, who has walked beside me
'On the road to Ballybay'.

Tones That Are Tender
Percy French
1854 – 1920

Berrie O'Neill

Percy French Society
in association with
The Lilliput Press

First published in 2016 by The Lilliput Press, Dublin
This edition published in 2022 by The Lilliput Press, Dublin

© Copyright Berrie O'Neill, 2016, 2022
www.lilliputpress.ie

All rights reserved. No part of this book may be reproduced, stored in or introduced into a retrieval system, or transmitted in any form or by any means (electronic, mechanical, photocopying, recording or otherwise) without the permission of the publishers and copyright owners.

ISBN 978-1-843-51856-3

Set in 11pt/14pt Minion Pro Roman and Minion Pro italics

Front: Montage of original letters, illustration by E.K. French, cover of *The Jarvey*, watercolour by Percy French, drawing of Cloonyquin by Raymond Piper and photograph of Percy French

Back: Montage of three song covers 'Phil the Fluter's Ball', 'The Night Miss Cooney Eloped' and 'Slattery's Mounted Fut'

Printed in the Czech Republic by Finidr

Design: Jonny Kane, Belfast

CONTENTS

Foreword	7
Preamble	9
Introduction	13
1. A Brief Historical Perspective	15
2. Ancestral Voices	16
3. Childhood at Cloonyquin: Early Influences	24
4. Difficult Times: 'The Stranded Gentry'!	29
5. The 'Baleful Influence'	32
6. The Magic Spell	35
7. An Early Literary Contribution	42
8. 'The world and we were in our prime once, only once, upon a time'	45
9. His 'Ray of Sunshine'	56
10. Songs from the 1880s	61
11. The 'Jarvey' Years	64
12. The Old Curiosity Shop	74
13. Triumph and Tragedy	78
14. Life Goes On, As It Must	84
15. Helen (Lennie) Sheldon	87
16. The Professional Entertainer	91
17. The West Clare Railway	96
18. 'This London's a Wonderful Sight'	98
19. Towards the Peak of His Career	102

20.	Songs, Satires and Spells	107
21.	Celestial Painting	112
22.	Smoke Painting and Other Unusual Artistic Skills	115
23.	'Across the Atlantical Sea'	117
24.	'Tones That Are Tender and Tones That Are Gruff'	125
25.	'He Loved the Old Country and Its People'	127
26.	Oh Switzerland!	134
27.	The Changing Scene	137
28.	The Challenges of Wartime	139
29.	'When the Story's Nearly Ended'	143
	Epilogue	146
	Memorial Fund	155
	As Others Remembered Him	157
	The Percy French Collection	159
	Acknowledgments	168
	Bibliography	170
	Index of Persons and Places	171

FOREWORD

I would like to thank Berrie O'Neill for asking me to provide this Foreword to his most excellent tribute to my great-uncle. For a very long time there has been a distinct need for a proper biography of Percy French. And here it is, at last. Berrie has done a wonderful amount of detailed work in researching the history of the French family. And I, for one, have learnt a tremendous lot about my French ancestors – and my Uncle Willie.

Sadly I never knew Willie, but I have many happy memories of his second wife, Lennie, and their three daughters – and of wonderful times spent at 130 Hamilton Terrace in St John's Wood (where they lived for many years) and then in Monks Eleigh, where they moved after the Second World War.

It is wonderful to think that Uncle Willie's work is kept alive by the various Percy French Societies in Ireland – particularly the excellent Percy French Society that emerged in North Down in 1983, which owns a huge archive of memorabilia and paintings and has given rise to others in Roscommon, Galway and Co. Leitrim. I must not forget the late, great Brendan O'Dowda (who started the Percy French renaissance with his recordings of many of the songs, and the one-man show he toured for many years) and Alan Tongue, with his ground breaking TV programme, and then his book, with its illustrations and pithy comments. I am so grateful to everyone who has been responsible for keeping my Uncle Willie's name in the spotlight.

Courtney Kenny

A Lavish Prodigality

His watercolours of Ireland, flung out with a lavish prodigality, bestowed upon friends, or sold or a song, are – now that the incessantly-working hand is stilled – coming into their own. He would arrive at a house unexpectedly early, ask for a table, chair, and glass of water, begin painting the things he had seen – the wonderful colours of the bogs and the distant mountains covered with heather, the white-walled gold thatched cottage by the side of the bog-pool; the little trees with their feet in the bogs. Overhead the soft and tumbled cloud through the chinks in which the light came raining. He is the interpreter of still life, land and skyscape in Western Ireland.

Katherine Tynan
Foreword to Chronicles and Poems of Percy French

A Kindly Act

In 1916 Mr and Mrs Bell and their children, Willie, Cecil, Robert and Mary, together with their little friend, Tommy Sfockdale visited Newcastle, Co. Down on the August Bank Holiday, from their home in Downpatrick. Mr Bell, an exceptionally strong swimmer, having spent some time teaching the boys, went for a swim on his own.

Soon, however, the boys noticed that their father was not making progress. Alarmed, they turned and saw a man in the sand dunes looking out to sea through binoculars. Percy French, the man with the binoculars, confirmed that the swimmer was indeed in trouble. He went to the Slieve Donard Hotel to raise the alarm but alas Mr Bell was already dead from apoplexy.

In 1994, Mr Bell's daughter, Mary (then Mrs Small), recalled that Percy French had provided a watercolour for auction to help the distressed widow and her family. Some time later he called at their fruit and vegetable shop in Downpatrick and gave her mother some tickets for his next performance. Mary recalled him singing 'Come Back Paddy Reilly' but it was his paintings that fascinated her the most.

The Jarvey,
Newsletter of the Percy French Society

PREAMBLE

Biography, once an exercise in solemn sanctification, is now robust and irreverent – and all the better for it. Yet we should not be afraid to admire our subjects.

Peter J. Conradi

Amongst other interesting comments in his text *The Art of Biography*, Peter J. Conradi states, 'The good biography is one in which those "on the other side" are successfully induced after arduous research and by dint of sheer writerly enchantment to appear to walk and talk again so that we can enjoy their company and, perhaps, even learn from their mistakes'.

*Could I find again the woodland
Where I loved to lie and dream,
While the dragon flies were dancing
To the rippling of the stream.*

*I'd give up all the world has brought
And all that it may bring,
To be that merry boy again,
Sailing through the Spring.*

Lines from Percy French's poem 'Retrospection'.

William Percy French (the name given to him at birth) was 'Willie' to his family and in his earlier years as student, civil engineer, journalist, songwriter and artist variously 'W. French', 'W.P. French', 'William Percy French' or 'W. Percy French' (as is etched on the grave stone of his first wife, Ethel Armytage Moore). By the time he went to live in London *c.*1900 he had changed it to 'Percy French'. Only exceptionally do we find him referred to as 'Percy', mostly by those not well known to him. To professional friends like Dr Houston Collisson he was merely 'French', as would have been the custom of the time and which will often be used in this study.

Cloonyquin (beautiful meadows) was located deep in the Co. Roscommon countryside, not too far from the ancient village of Tulsk and within four or five miles of both the Cathedral town of Elphin and the more modern landlord-designed town of Strokestown.

Mrs De Burgh Daly (Emily Lucy French) was a younger sister of William Percy French. She was the editor and the most important contributor to *Chronicles and Poems of Percy French*, published in 1922 shortly after the death in 1920 of her brother. Soon afterwards she edited *Prose, Poems and Parodies of Percy French*.

Ettie French (Ettie Percy French) was the eldest of three daughters of William Percy French by his second marriage. She was the author of *Willie*, a tribute to her father written when she was aged ninety-five and published by the Percy French Society in 1993.

∙ ∙ ∙ ∙ ∙ ∙ ∙ ∙ ∙ ∙ ∙

Live within my income?
Very much I doubt it;
What I'd like to know is
How to live without it.

Tones That Are Tender
Percy French
1854 – 1920

INTRODUCTION

It is a major task to do justice to another account of the life of one who is already acknowledged to have brought laughter and enjoyment to so many people during his life as a civil engineer, journalist, author, poet, parodist, artist, songwriter and entertainer. Apart from the invaluable *Chronicles and Poems of Percy French* edited by Mrs De Burgh Daly (sister of Percy French) there are also significant biographical-type publications by three of his greatest disciples, James N. Healy with *Percy French and His Songs*, Brendan O'Dowda with *The World of Percy French* and Alan Tongue's *A Picture of Percy French*. James N. Healy and Brendan O'Dowda were notable performers of Percy French's songs and recitations; Alan Tongue was mostly involved in the production and direction of a series of programmes and documentaries for television. All three were devoted and enthusiastic admirers of the man and his works and all have enjoyed the confidence of his then surviving daughters, Ettie and Joan French.

Watercolour by Percy French

'O'er moor and fen, o'er crag and torrent,'

John H. Newman

Words etched on the gravestone of Percy French at St Luke's Churchyard, Formby, Merseyside

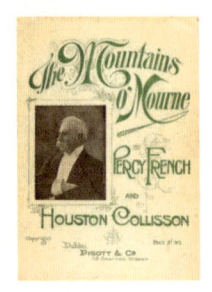

Song cover

The Percy French Collection, North Down Museum

But, maybe a more complete picture can yet be elicited. What for instance is the ancestry and full family background of one who is often described in simplified terms as a Protestant son of an Irish landlord or sometimes, on the other hand, as Renaissance man? What combination of talents, personality and life experience would find him equally at home either with the audience in a small hall in the west of Ireland or entertaining members of the English royal family in their Sandringham home? What are the ingredients of songs that, despite the prolific output of the modern highly geared song publishing industry, continue to be enjoyed almost a century after the composer's death? Just what is it that makes his simple but prolifically produced watercolour sketches ever more collectable? And, less seriously perhaps, why are the beams in the roof of a well-known hostelry in Donaghadee, Co. Down the only place where the name of Percy French can be seen grouped with such unquestioned literary greats W.B. Yeats, Oscar Wilde and James Joyce?

'Evening Sunlight'

Watercolour by Percy French

Courtesy of Gladys O'Neill

1. A BRIEF HISTORICAL PERSPECTIVE

The Normans

'Nearly sixty years ago an event of immense importance occurred in the history of Ireland'. Writing from the later years of his life, this is how Percy French reflected on his birth in his introduction to the book *Chronicles and Poems of Percy French* compiled and edited by his sister, Mrs De Burgh Daly. In typical style he headlines the story in historic terms but goes on to give it an ironic, anticlimactic twist: 'No cables buzzed the news to the ends of the earth. No telephones rang – there were none to ring.' It is an example of a characteristic aspect of Percy French's writings, in which the sensational or the grandiose is reduced to the ordinary and the routine by an ironic, comic or sometimes satirical view of the world. His distrust of the ostentatious and the overblown was a hallmark of much of his varied literary and journalistic output.

But perhaps we may be allowed to begin with a really momentous but much earlier 'event of immense importance in the history of Ireland.' A philosophical friend often used to say: 'I wonder what might have happened if the Normans had not come to Ireland'. And so well he might, as surely one of the really significant turning points in Irish history was the conquest of most of Ireland in the twelfth and thirteenth centuries by the Anglo-Normans. It was an event that came about with the initial blessing of the one and only English Pope, Adrian IV, who gave King Henry II an excuse to invade Ireland. The plan was to establish more control over an apparently misbehaving Irish church.

This strategy was helped on its way through the collusion of the recently ousted king of Leinster Diarmait MacMurchada (Dermot MacMurrough). Being much in need of military assistance to regain his kingdom, he gave his daughter Aoife (Eva) in marriage to Richard de Clare, usually known as Strongbow, 2nd Earl of Pembroke and one of the most powerful Norman knights.

'The Marriage of Strongbow and Aoife'

Artist:
Daniel MacLise
Irish, c.1854

Oil on canvas, unframed:
315cm x 513cm

Photo: National Gallery of Ireland

The wedding arising from this apparently mutually suitable arrangement (we cannot know whether Aoife was consulted) was a historic occasion, celebrated with much hospitality. 'The Marriage of Strongbow and Aoife' is the subject of a magnificent painting in oils by one of Ireland's most distinguished artists, Daniel MacLise.

Whether because the painting of Daniel MacLise influenced him or because he had studied the history of Strongbow and the Norman background to his French family name, the story of Strongbow and his wedding would in due course be satirized by Percy French in a comic opera named *Strongbow*. In French's version of Strongbow's wedding, the best man, for instance, mistakes a spirit licence for a wedding licence, a small example of French's early humour in his farcical version of the famous wedding. But, sadly, his operatic work came to an untimely end in the face of critical comment that it was founded on an event in Irish history that should not be so lightly treated. Amongst other things French's libretto portrayed the Normans as having been 'invited' to Ireland – too close maybe to the truth for the comfort of the historians of the time. Happily, however, his involvement in the *Strongbow* operetta would in the following years have another and more important outcome.

These images of the wedding celebrations expose a degree of human weakness and most likely give a less than balanced impression of Strongbow, 2nd Earl of Pembroke, whose burial place is in the ancient Christ Church Cathedral in Dublin and whose effigy is prominent there today. It is not of course the task of these brief paragraphs to examine the extent to which the church in Ireland improved after the inevitably rather bloody invasion. But Strongbow, his associates and descendants, no doubt thanks to their acknowledged military and organisational skills, consolidated and grew their lordship and influence in Ireland whilst constructing notable and lasting seats of power in strategic places such as Carrickfergus, Kilkenny, Trim and Dundrum (Co. Down). They also built monasteries, churches and the tower houses that still dominate our landscape today.

The Normans intermarried with the noble Gaelic families, grew in power and wealth and are said, with only a degree of exaggeration, to have become 'more Irish than the Irish themselves'. We may still be familiar with family names such as FitzSimons, de Cogan, FitzGerald, de Burgh, de Courcy, D'Arcy, Power and French (an anglicized version of De Freyne).

Carrickfergus Castle, Co. Antrim

Twelfth century stronghold of John de Courcy

2. ANCESTRAL VOICES

In time the descendants of some of those twelfth- and thirteenth-century Norman arrivals in Ireland became part of the famous mercantile elite of Galway city where an original fort had been captured by the powerful Norman knight Sir Richard De Burgo in 1235. Between the thirteenth and seventeenth centuries these Galway families, most of whom were of Norman–English or Norman–Welsh origins, became wealthy and powerful through trading with France, Spain and the West Indies. Part of what is sometimes defined as the old English gentry, they had acquired commercial and trading privileges within the walls of the city of Galway – privileges guaranteed by municipal charter from the English government. This mercantile elite, led by the Lynch dynasty and including the Frenches, had for long shared social, political and municipal power in the city of Galway until, being naturally royalist in outlook, they fell foul of Cromwell's uncompromising parliamentarian ideals in the seventeenth century. Indeed, the title 'Tribes of Galway' by which they became known was bestowed on them by Oliver Cromwell himself and not intended to be complimentary.

In due course many of the civic fortunes earned by these families were invested in the acquisition of lands and the building of mighty tower houses and mansions. In the publication *Galway History and Society*, a chapter on the 'Galway Tribes as Landowners and Gentry' notes that by the eighteenth century the French dynasty owned over twenty houses and estates in the counties Galway, Mayo and Roscommon. Some of these were relatively small but five major estates had continuity from the seventeenth to the twentieth centuries. At 50,000 acres, the largest of these was Tyrone outside Galway city, an estate which, it is understood, was gradually built up through a combination of purchase and what is described as 'good marriages, sometimes with Protestant families'. At a mere 3000 acres, the smallest of those five major estates was Cloonyquin, Co. Roscommon, which Arthur French of Tyrone (mayor of Galway in 1691) purchased towards the end of the seventeenth century.

In the eventful year of 1691 Mayor Arthur French not only found the city besieged by the Williamite army but also contracted his second marriage. He married Sarah Burke (widow of one Iriel Farrell), the only child of Ulick Burke of Claregalway (Burke being of course a derivation of the Norman name, De Burgh or De Burgo). This marriage and the acquisition of the Cloonyquin estate, together with the continuation of the Tyrone family through the progeny of Arthur and his first wife, Mary Kirwin, ensured that Arthur French set in train two more or less separate lines of this notable 'French' dynasty. But it is the Cloonyquin line that will be the focus of our story.

Abbey of Claregalway by W.H. Bartlett, 1809-54

The Cloonyquin Estate

It was a time in Ireland when after the Williamite wars the Penal Laws, which had been designed partly to prevent the Roman Catholic aristocracy from owning land, were still influencing the acquisition of property. In the circumstances some Catholic landlords conformed to the established church (the Church of Ireland) to avoid the loss or fragmentation of their estates. In the case of the aforesaid estate of Cloonyquin, the purchaser, Arthur French, sent his eldest son from his second marriage (also Arthur French) to a Protestant school in Kilkenny so that the son could hold the newly acquired Cloonyquin estate in his own name. This (second) Arthur French of Cloonyquin, High Sheriff of Roscommon, married Judith Davis of Carrickfergus in 1715 and begat four sons, the eldest being the third Arthur French.

Although born at Cloonyquin this third bearer of the 'Arthurian' name, who owned the Cloonyquin estate from 1729 to 1789, is understood to have lived mainly in London and appears to have been an early example of the absentee Irish landlord. According to Ettie French (daughter of Percy French), in her memoir *Willie*, when Arthur returned at some point from London he found the original 'big house' (known locally as 'the Castle') burnt down. We know not whether he was in any way shocked or taken aback to find his home in ashes. He must have resolved to forsake 'absentee' status because he extended the dimensions of the house that was built as the estate shooting lodge to become a more modest Cloonyquin residence for himself and subsequent generations.

John French (1764-1823): The Spanish Connection

Having seemingly settled at Cloonyquin, the third Arthur French did not marry. The estate passed first to his nephew, Henry Walter French, who had no children, and then to another nephew, John French, son of Arthur's youngest brother, Christopher. From the French family tree impressively compiled by Sir Alfred Irwin in 1912 we learn that John's father, Christopher French (great-great-grandfather of Percy French) lived a colourful life: '22nd Regt. 1743-1777; Lt.Col. 52nd Regt. 1777. Served in the wars in America and the West Indies. b. about 1725. d. June 1797. m. 1748, Margarita Alberti, at Minorca.'

When writing about Christopher French, one Sheldon S. Cohen, Professor of History at Loyola University Chicago, discovered that Captain French (as he was then known) had served in the American Revolution. He was held captive in Hartford, Connecticut for over a year before escaping. Apparently his journals and letters to and from George Washington are preserved in the Library of Congress. Later in his career, while serving in Minorca with his regiment, Christopher (by then Lt. Col.) fell in love with a beautiful girl he had seen through the gates of a convent. Several clandestine meetings followed before he and a fellow soldier who had formed a liaison with another student nun got both ladies out of a convent window and went straight to a church to be married. It is pleasing to read that Margarita survived her husband Christopher by five months after fifty years of 'blissful marriage.'

It is worth noting at this point that Margarita's place in the evolution of the French family was honoured; it is known that one of Percy French's nieces was named Maeve Pauline Alberti French. Her first name, Maeve, can also be interpreted as a sign of a family awareness of an older culture. The mound of Rathcroghan, the ancient burial place of the Kings of Connaught under which it is believed lies the palace of Queen Maeve, is visible from the Cloonyquin homestead. Maeve was destined in time to be mother of the notable pianist, entertainer and opera director, Courtney Kenny, one time Musical Director at the Bristol Old Vic and later, Head of the Music Staff at the Wexford Festival of Opera.

Rathcroghan, ancient burial place of the Kings of Connaught

Though Cloonyquin is located deep in the countryside of Co. Roscommon, it can be deduced from the family tree that the family was very much involved in the social and governmental scene of a nineteenth-century Ireland that was still firmly part of the United Kingdom of Great Britain and Ireland. This was reflected in the family members' careers and marriages, which were sometimes contracted beyond the confines of these islands. It was quite the norm for the second, third or fourth sons of landed families to find careers in the armies of the British Empire. Like his father Christopher, John French, who had inherited the Cloonyquin estate, is described as 'Capt. 4th D. G. 1799, Major 121st Foot, Lt.Col. in Army, 1831, Qr.-Master Gen, under Sir G. Murray in Holland, b. 23 June, 1764. d. 1823. m. June, 1789, Ann, da. of the Ven. Joseph Story, Archdeacon of Kilmore.'

William Christopher St George French (1790-1852)

William Christopher St George French (1790-1852) of Cloonyquin was the eldest of John and Ann French's seven children. He was High Sheriff of Roscommon in 1827 and he also appears to have combined his army career (22nd Regt. 6th D.G.) with local government involvement. Interestingly, in the context of this story of (William) Percy French, this is the first use of the name William in the family tree. In her memoir *Willie*, ninety-five-year-old Ettie French writes:

> When William came to Cloonyquin he brought with him a well-endowed bride. He put a Regency frill across the front of the house creating another mixture of periods, but actually pulling the house together outside. The effect from the inside of two long rooms rather openly divided and their five large windows, was somehow very welcoming. The first room contained the library which William had brought with him, and it was here that 'Willie' [her father], who learned to read at an early age, found his inspiration for the various sailors on the pond.

The 'well-endowed' bride brought by William to Cloonyquin in 1819 was Dorothea Helen Harris, daughter of Michael Harris, resident of 9 Upper Merrion Street Dublin and attorney of Eden, Rathfarnham. It seems very likely that the 'well-endowed' Dorothea Helen Harris brought substantial, and probably necessary, monetary support to Cloonyquin. This may have been what enabled the house to be further extended and, for all we know, may have brought other less materialistic endowments as well. But above all Dorothea should be given credit as grandmother to Percy French, the subject of our story. What is significant in the above quote is not only Ettie French's reference to an imaginative game played on the pond at the rear of Cloonyquin (which Percy French would mention much later in his nostalgic poem 'Retrospection') but also her reference to the library, the books which would play a vital part in the educational, imaginative and literary development of her father.

William Percy French (1854-1920)

Christopher French J.P., D.L. of Cloonyquin (1821-1897) and High Sheriff of Roscommon, inherited the estate from his father, William Christopher St George French, and in 1851 married Susan Emma, daughter of the Rev. Wm. Alex Percy, Rector of Kiltoghert, Carrick-on-Shannon, Co. Leitrim. Their first child, Elizabeth Jane French (1851-1906) was unmarried and ownership of Cloonyquin descended to their first son, Arthur John St. George French, J.P., described in Sir Alfred Irwin's French family tree as 'Major, North Staffordshire Regt., High Sheriff of Roscommon 1902.'

The second son of Christopher French and Susan Percy arrived on 1 May 1854, once regarded as the first day of summer. With its ancient inspirations for festivals and celebrations, May Day could be considered a felicitous birthday for William Percy French, the new arrival to Cloonyquin. He would go on to bring joy not only to his parents but also to audiences on these islands and sometimes beyond.

Christopher French 1821-97

Father of William Percy French

The Percy French Collection, North Down Museum

Christopher French
of Mulpit & Tyrone, Co. Galway
m. Jane
|
Arthur French
of Tyrone Co. Galway
& Cloonyquin
m. Sarah Burke *1691*
|
Arthur French
of Cloonyquin, High Sheriff
m. Judith Davis *1715*
|
Christopher French
c. 1725 – 1797
m. Margarita Alberti *1748*
|
John French
of Cloonyquin
1764 – 1823
m. Ann Story *1789*
|
William Christopher
St George French
of Cloonyquin, High Sheriff
1790 – 1852
m. Dorothea Helen Harris *1819*
|
Christopher French
Cloonyquin, J.P., D.L., High Sheriff
1821 – 1897
m. Susan Emma Percy 1851

Elizabeth Jane	Arthur John St George	William Percy	Dorothea Emma	Alice Kathleen	Emily Lucy	Henry Percy	Christine Laura Sophie	Christopher St George
b. 1851	b.1853	b.1854	b.1855	b.1857	b.1859	b.1863	b.1869	b.1872

3. CHILDHOOD AT CLOONYQUIN: EARLY INFLUENCES

We are mostly dependent to the editorship and authorship of Mrs De Burgh Daly (i.e. Emily Lucy French, sister of Percy French) together with the reflections of Percy French himself in *Chronicles and Poems of Percy French* for information on Christopher French, his wife Susan and their nine children's lives at Cloonyquin. Even allowing for a degree of nostalgia and sepia-shaded memories, everything in their writings points to a happy and healthy, but rather protected and restricted, family environment in which Percy French and his siblings would develop and grow.

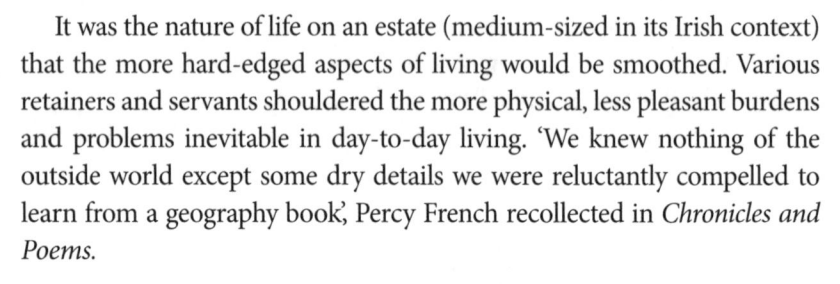

It was the nature of life on an estate (medium-sized in its Irish context) that the more hard-edged aspects of living would be smoothed. Various retainers and servants shouldered the more physical, less pleasant burdens and problems inevitable in day-to-day living. 'We knew nothing of the outside world except some dry details we were reluctantly compelled to learn from a geography book', Percy French recollected in *Chronicles and Poems*.

Though he mentions in his reflections that the library at Cloonyquin was 'much above the book collections of the average country house', French clearly enjoyed stories of high adventure more than the classical authors favoured by his Oxford-educated father. Whilst tutors and governesses came and went at intervals, he found the learning they imparted 'a fearful bore.' However, the Rev. James Rountree – whom Percy French describes as 'his friend and tutor' – left an indelible, if not entirely welcome, mark on his pupil. He introduced French to Euclid with some success. This accomplishment of sorts set him on his way to being burdened (as he saw it) with the epithet of 'mathematical scholar', a remark that would fuel his father's unrelenting pursuit of an engineering career for his second son.

Susan French
The Percy French Collection, North Down Museum

Childhood at Cloonyquin: Early Influences

'Cloonyquin'

Watercolour by Percy French

Courtesy of Courtney Kenny

Mention of tutors and governesses is another signpost of life in a 'big house.' Here it is appropriate to note a comment once made to this writer by the late Seamus De Nash, whose forebears were neighbours or maybe tenants of the French family. Seamus spoke of how neighbouring children, including his grandfather, were happily allowed to attend and share in the educational output of the tutors employed for the benefit of the French children. Mrs De Burgh Daly confirms that her father's great interest in education extended to his tenants and that there were two schools on the estate.

Boyhood life for Willie at Cloonyquin was wholesome but 'rather strict', to use his own words. Adherence to religious observance was confined to Sundays when morning prayers were held; church service was attended; and, after a 'substantial Sunday dinner', there followed a long walk with visits to some of the tenants. There is no record of any strong negative reaction by him to the family ban on books of a secular nature on Sundays, but the discipline of church going caused a degree of frustration, albeit couched in typically humorous vein. To begin with, it was a four or five mile drive by carriage or car to Elphin Cathedral for worship. For the young boy to sustain himself through the ordeal of Dean and

Mrs Warburton's services required that he prepare by 'filling his pockets with gooseberries or whatever portable food was in season'. Even allowing for his *Chronicles* writings being in retrospect, the following memories are expressed in trenchant style. We have in them an early indication that the young boy, then called Willie French, possessed a critical mind:

> [Mrs Warburton] was choir and organist combined, and it was many years before I discovered that church music was anything but a duet between a high-pitched soprano and the local policeman who growled an octave lower. The sermon was generally of that style of oratory which consists of putting up a row of utterly untenable doctrines and then knocking them down one by one.

One notable aspect of studies of the works of Percy French is the total absence of any reference to religious faith or church matters. Whether here in his youthful views on his church attendance or in his resistance to the classical literature favoured by his father, there are unmistakeable signs of the boy thinking outside the accepted parameters of the comfortable conformity into which he was born. Many years later his daughter Ettie would add further insight: 'Willie was never a churchman, perhaps owing to his mother's rather severe version of Church of Ireland procedure. However, he was truly reverent: I never heard him take the name of the Lord in vain.'

Mrs De Burgh Daly is on record as saying, 'Our father was an extremely intellectual man, a classical scholar to the end of his days. He took a great interest in his tenants and in county work, and was a man of most liberal views in many ways.' It is generally accepted that the French family of Cloonyquin have always been regarded as 'good' landlords, although it is more than likely that their 'goodness' or humane treatment of tenants would have had a negative effect on the wealth of the estate. Nonetheless, good relationships and an all round respect for people of all creeds and classes emerge as distinguishing marks of the Christopher French era at Cloonyquin. While inevitably remaining in their own place in keeping with the context, servants and retainers come across as equals in human terms.

Childhood at Cloonyquin: Early Influences

Always, it seems, with an ear for a rhyme or a song, Percy French recalls with much clarity how 'the servants gave him a bit of a lilt' – the cook's contribution had something akin to a biblical flavour:

> *Three angels at their station*
> *All deep in conversation,*
> *All takin' recreation*
> *All by the Baltic Say.*
>
> *Tis Mark and Luke and Matcha*
> *That's sittin' there to watcha*
> *For fear the Divil catcha*
> *All by the Baltic Say.*

Song cover
The Percy French Collection, North Down Museum

Indeed a tiny seed of Percy French's subsequent career may be contained in these rhymes. This is evidenced when with World War I underway some fifty years later in 1914, French, by then an established songwriter, wrote the song 'All by the Baltic Say'. It is a kind of light-hearted, long drawn-out ridicule of the Kaiser Wilhelm and the German army but also contains a very prescient verse: 'For men who go to battle/Like droves of driven cattle/Feel bad when bullets rattle/All by the Baltic Say.' One might nowadays argue that though in 1914 he had no hint of the nightmares to come, French's image of 'droves of driven cattle' was in a small way ahead of younger war poets, such as Wilfred Owen or Donegal man, Patrick MacGill. So step forward the lilting cook at Cloonyquin and take a belated bow for her possible 'pebble in a pool' influence. And who knows what 'Old Maginnis, the coachman' may have started, with the worldly tale of 'Red-headed Reilly and tatterin' Jack':

> *Oh! red-headed Reilly and tatterin' Jack*
> *Wandherin' over the world and back;*
> *Terrible rogues for stealin' the pogues*
> *Was red-headed Reilly and tatterin' Jack.*

It is likely that the young Willie French had a closer philosophical affinity with the cook and the coachman than with Dean Warburton. He would never admit, one feels, to such a judgement without assuaging the thought with a touch of humour. Christopher, his classically educated father, was not bereft of a sense of the comic himself despite the weight of scholarship. Percy French recalls how his father once, rather surprisingly, sang the chorus of a comic song:

> *She was very fond of dancing,*
> *But allow me to remark*
> *That one fine day*
> *She danced away*
> *With a calico printer's clerk!*

For young 'Willie', who in later life would sometimes be referred to as a composer of comic songs, the extent of the combined influence of his father, the cook and the coachman should not be underestimated. But let us also remember the words of his sister Emily (Mrs De Burgh Daly): 'Our mother … one of the beautiful Miss Percys … They were … extremely witty and musical as well as good-looking.'

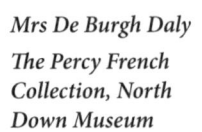

Mrs De Burgh Daly
The Percy French Collection, North Down Museum

4. DIFFICULT TIMES: 'THE STRANDED GENTRY'!

Overall, in the early years of Percy French's childhood and education one senses an unchanging pattern in the Cloonyquin way of life. This is notwithstanding the fact that the problems of land ownership and distribution in Ireland throughout the nineteenth century were manifested in what historians term 'agrarian violence', much of which was directed against the landlords and their agents. Although the effects of the awful famine of the 1840s were still in living memory and much blame was being laid at the door of the landlords, relationships between landlord and tenant were, as far as can be ascertained, extraordinarily respectful at Cloonyquin. This is maybe surprising when looked at beside the happenings at a much larger estate and mansion nearby at Strokestown Park where the landlord Denis Mahon was assassinated in 1847. In her memoir *Willie*, Ettie French quotes a former tenant's letter to Cloonyquin, written in the USA long after the infamous famine: 'you made all your tenants happy. The one that had a bad house you repaired for him, the family that was hungry you fed them'.

Photo courtesy of Strokestown Park, Co. Roscommon, now the Irish National Famine Museum

'Cloonyquin'

Pencil drawing by Raymond Piper, F.L.S., R.U.A., U.W.S.

Courtesy of Berrie O'Neill

In the face of changing social, economic and political forces, the era of the 'big house' of whatever dimension (if the Cloonyquin 'shooting lodge' was modest, the Strokestown Palladian-style mansion was magnificent) was declining from its great days. It is partly a matter of speculation as to how these outside trends affected the young Willie French. Upon hearing that the family were included in *Burke's Landed Gentry*, French later remarked ruefully that 'stranded gentry' would have been a more appropriate description. This remark by the mature Percy French is yet another example of deeper feelings cloaked in a witticism or even having become the stimulus for a joke. The family at Cloonyquin must have been aware of certain worrying signs. Mrs De Burgh Daly writes of being warned not to be out late, of police patrols in the grounds and of the quaint practice of 'burying the plate', a precaution against losing valuable family silver. Whether or not the Cloonyquin 'plate' was worth burying is unclear, but the young Willie would jokingly suggest doing it on cold winter nights when the ground was 'like a stone'. Willie himself wrote of those worries: 'There was war between landlord and tenant in those days, but beyond a wandering agent who turned up to lunch with a brace of pistols sticking out of his pockets, we (children) knew nothing of it.'

Later, when French was aged about twenty and already possessed a deducible literary bent, he first edited a fun family magazine 'The Tulsk Morning Howl' (handwritten and illustrated with his own drawings), and then the equally ironically named 'The Trombone of Truth'. The 'Trombone' includes light-hearted accounts of holidays in Bundoran and hunting with the local harriers. One edition contained a parody of the 'Who Killed Cock Robin?' nursery rhyme, which began:

> *Who shot the agent?*
> *'I' said the thrush,*
> *'With an ould Blunderbush,*
> *I shot the agent.'*
>
> *Who saw him die?*
> *'I' said the fly,*
> *(I know it's a lie)*
> *'I saw him die.'*

A summer number of 'The Trombone of Truth'

The Percy French Collection, North Down Museum

And amongst a number of other verses:

> *Who got around the Editor?*
> *'I' said the rook,*
> *'I can talk like a book,*
> *I got around the Editor.'*

The parody was based on the account of the murder of a land agent that appeared in a well-established daily newspaper only to be contradicted in the next day's edition. The parody with sentences such as the colloquial 'Who got around the Editor?' is obviously and critically reacting against perceived and undue influences being at work but is also evidence of an underlying violence in the area of land agitation.

The very titles of the family magazines, 'The Tulsk Morning Howl' and 'The Trombone of Truth', are ironic in concept, suggesting a blaring forth of something less than the truth. The parody of 'Cock Robin' demonstrates that, even in those early days, a critical mind was already at work, its criticism cloaked in humorous verse.

5. THE 'BALEFUL INFLUENCE'

We learn from Mrs De Burgh Daly that her (and Percy French's) father did not believe in sending boys under ten-years-old to boarding school. Hence the presence of tutors in Cloonyquin as already mentioned. But, eventually, the time came for young Willie French's future to be faced. Writing retrospectively of this crucial time, Percy French relates how at the ripe old age of ten, after his strict upbringing, he probably longed for a little less restraint. So, when his mother, a 'kind and gentle lady', enquired as to what he should like to be, he promptly replied that he 'would like to be a pirate.' This, he wrote, with perhaps a degree of understatement, was a shock to his mother (who had hoped he would enter the Church).

Parnell at Westminster

At this juncture, his father suggested that his son should be made a lawyer – something Percy French describes in *Chronicles* as being somewhere between a pirate and a clergyman! Notwithstanding this clever and amusing account, there had begun to emerge a dilemma for Percy French. Traditionally for his kind of 'landed' family, careers in the army or the Church were the norm for second or subsequent sons, with professional careers in law or engineering there as alternatives to the dreaded possibility of being 'in trade.' Much later in his unorthodox career, Percy French would be free to demolish attitudes that had become outdated, as indicated in the first verse of his poem 'Things that Matter':

> *Father's lost all the money he made,*
> *I think it's the best bit of fun,*
> *He says I must go into trade*
> *And make bricks, like my gran'papa done.*

An English education was probably *de rigueur* for families of landlords, even 'stranded' ones. Eventually, aged ten, young Willie found himself at a preparatory school at Kirk Langley in Derbyshire, where Charles Stewart Parnell preceded him by some years. Parnell, from a similar social background and one of the first pupils of the school, would in time achieve fame and controversy as MP and leader of the Irish Parliamentary Party at Westminster.

It is unlikely that the Kirk Langley experience had a lot to do with the future careers of either pupil but Parnell was even more at odds with the preparatory school at Kirk Langley than Willie French. According to Willie, the headmaster's wife, 'dear old Mrs Barton', taught drawing not very well. Her daughter made more of an impact on him by teaching him that kissing outside the family circle 'can be quite a delightful pastime'. The more lasting outcome of the Kirk Langley experience however was the further promulgation of the myth of young Willie as a potential mathematical genius. The knowledge of Euclid imparted by his former tutor, James Rountree, had put him so far ahead of the other boys, who had not yet even attempted the subject, that the headmaster wrote to his father, 'Your son, for his age, is quite the finest mathematical scholar we have ever had!' A conclusion that, Percy French claimed, 'exercised a most baleful influence over my whole life'.

Aged thirteen or thereabouts, young Willie found himself at Windermere College in the English Lake District. We know little of his academic development, if any, during his three or four years at this establishment that nowadays no longer exists. The headmaster, with the unusual name of George Hale Puckle, had acquired some kind of mathematical reputation through an academic work on the esoteric subject of Conic Sections. This reputation encouraged Willie's father to give his son further opportunity to fulfil the paternal dream and grand design of an engineering future.

There is little doubt at this point that the young Willie was rebelling against the mathematical genius myth that was preceding him. He writes in slightly ironic terms that he never got to know what Conic Sections were or did, but that by his second term he had become champion fives player. This suggests that the academic side was all a waste of time. The masters were 'remote tyrants' who, for instance, were oblivious to certain strange rites being practised in the school by some of the more esoteric students. 'It is wonderful how little you can learn if you take no interest in any of your studies' is a quotation that is further suggestive of one completely at odds with what was on offer at Windermere College.

Masthead from 'Our School Times', c.1880

Percy French Society Archives

A few of his rather impertinent exchanges with the teachers and his resulting boxed ears are a likely outcome of his frustration. Strangely, but maybe in line with the times in which he lived and the Cloonyquin ethos, there is no record of young Willie protesting to his father (who had not lost his unwavering faith in the mathematical reputation of his son). With English education not quite measuring up, Willie found himself back in Ireland at Foyle College where, according to a fellow student John Ross (later Sir John Ross, Chancellor of Ireland) a relative of the French family, the Rev. Wm. P. Robinson, D.D. was headmaster. Sir John Ross remembered being an editor of *The Foyle College Magazine* and being helped by Willie, whose rapid sketches and drawings were a source of wonder and delight. Willie himself would recall how 'an eminent mathematician called Johnson' was requested to apply the finishing touch for entrance to Trinity College, Dublin. Despite little evidence of any enthusiasm by his pupil, Mr Johnson managed to 'build up a beautiful structure on the flimsiest foundation' and young Willie made it to university.

6. THE MAGIC SPELL

In 1872 W. French arrived at the ancient university of Trinity College Dublin, long seen as the university of what had become known as the 'Protestant Ascendancy'. An Engineering School had been opened in 1842, one of the first of its kind in the United Kingdom – a sign perhaps that the Industrial Revolution was having an impact on the more traditional approach to further education. Maybe in his determination to have his son become an engineer the young student's father was more aware of current trends than we have hitherto understood. However, it was necessary for W. French to earn his B.A. qualification before availing himself of the opportunities provided by the Engineering School and thereby fulfilling his father's grand design.

Photo courtesy of Percy French Collection North Down Museum

Little is recorded of the studies, lectures and examinations of the nine years spent by W. French at Trinity College Dublin. 'I think taking up the banjo, lawn tennis and watercolour painting, instead of Chemistry, Geology and the theory of strains, must have retarded my progress a good deal', he later wrote of his college days. Despite the incentives to study that surrounded him at the great seat of learning he was only fully enthused by an experience at the then newly opened Gaiety Theatre.

It was to Miss Annie Tremaine and company playing in Offenbach's operas that he went 'night after night' and where he wrote, 'Music held me with its magic spell.' As evidence of this awakening, he bought a banjo.

Buying a banjo was perhaps not the most likely musical reaction to Offenbach's operas. One suspects it had at least as much to do with the fashion of the time; even the Prince of Wales was taking banjo lessons. The blacked-up Christy's Minstrels were then fashionable and a major initial musical influence on W. French, who had long enjoyed the plantation songs of Stephen Foster (blacking-up was not then frowned upon). Later he transferred his affections to the pantomime principal boy, Miss Bessie Ludlow, singing 'Little Sweetheart, Come and Kiss Me'. Bessie, however, apparently loved another and the spell was broken. And so, despite everything, he began to study for an engineering degree.

University life meant that most of the restrictions of home and boarding school no longer frustrated French's natural unconventional instincts. What records exist show that he was a very welcome entertainer at parties both within and without the college. One of his student friends, L. A. 'Archie' West, recalled that French detested the rules that prevented undergraduates from remaining out late on most nights. So as not to be bound by this convention he would sometimes climb athletically over the high gate at the back entrance to TCD, 'even with his beloved banjo under his arm.' What emerges is an irrepressible penchant to entertain with music and song, a trait that history would prove to be no passing phase.

We also know that a piano became part of the furnishings in his rooms at the university. When his father came to visit, French and his roommate hid this extravagance by donning their gowns and standing with their backs to the instrument throughout what must have been a rather stilted social event! 'Archie' West and his family were both wealthy and hospitable, qualities that W. French did not allow to go a-begging – an aspect of his

Advertising poster, Christy's Minstrels

Percy French Society Archives

character that would be practised with a natural aptitude throughout much of his life. He would arrive at the West's home lightly lumbered with only a toothbrush and a banjo. On one occasion, Mrs West commented favourably on French's dress for an approaching church service, not realizing that he was attired in Archie's clothes.

Whilst at the ancient seat of learning, French's interest in the emerging game of lawn tennis involved the unlawful use of part of the Provost's garden as a tennis court. The garden was of course of much greater dimension a century ago and supported the Provost's cow; presumably he and his friend Milne, plus many others, were not immediately or obviously

A youthful W. French with banjo and Johnny Richardson, his cousin.

It was at Canon Richardson's home in Formby that French would die in January 1920.

Photo courtesy of Percy French Collection North Down Museum

visible. However, on one occasion after an altercation involving the cow they were evicted by one Dr Shaw and faced the wrath of the College Board. The episode is recorded and illustrated in the manuscript magazine 'The Trombone of Truth', taking the form of a parody of 'The Owl and the Pussy Cat'. The resultant 'Tale of Rapine and Violence', particularly verse two, is indicative of strong feelings in the two students:

> *But Shaw that owl*
> *That elderly fowl,*
> *Whose soul is with rancour replete,*
> *Was awfully wrath*
> *This Vandal and Goth*
> *Had invaded his silvan retreat.*
> *Men say his dark breast*
> *Is never at rest*
> *Unless he's engaged in some row*
> *It could not be endured*
> *So he went to the 'Board'*
> *With a grievance as big as the cow.*

'The Owl and the Pussy Cat'

This rather minor incident reflects a number of aspects of the character of W. French, the student: a respect for the newish game of lawn tennis, a negative reaction to authority and the ability to channel mild resentment into satirical verse. As the years passed there was less and less evidence of an interest in an engineering career. Indeed the world of the scientific was itself disposed of rather scathingly. His father, a classical scholar, French alleged, only knew that 'previous to the time of Galileo the sun had gone round the earth' – as if the great Galileo had manhandled it in the opposite direction!

So, with the help of 'that eminent grinder, Marmaduke Backhouse', but still having taken the longest time on record to get his degree in engineering, French concluded later in life: 'after various attempts on the part of governesses, tutors, schoolmasters and college Dons to prepare me for a diplomatic, a military and scientific career, I emerged at last from the portals of TCD admirably unfitted for any profession whatsoever!'

For, alas! The foundation was rotten,
I crossed on a cable of cram,
Oh dear! What a lot I've forgotten
Since passing my final exam!

Here, one might detect a slight sense of regret that he had been the victim of his father's somewhat blinkered attitude, that an engineering career was pushed upon him by a father with scant scientific knowledge or understanding. His sister Mrs De Burgh Daly found it curious that although their father was proud of his son's cleverness, the former never realised that it pointed to more than mere talent and that 'it did not dawn on him that such artistic talents should have received special encouragement and development.' In later years, 'W. French B.A., C.E.' thought that his university tutor might have done rather more for the freshman. For instance, he could have pointed out that by getting a refund from the Bursar through not availing himself of 'Commons' (already paid for by his father) and spending the money on 'real silk tights' for a 'fairy', French had been unfair to his 'dear old governor'. Things might have been worse perhaps had it not been that, 'luckily for me, a natural dislike of alcohol in every form, an inability to smoke without being violently sick, and a tendency to forget what were trumps at whist, kept me out of the society of the more Rackety Botany Babes' – presumably a group of students residing at the Botany Bay student quarters of the university and of apparently dubious lifestyle. However, despite his aversion to tobacco, the university 'smoking concerts' were a natural outlet for French's entertaining and musical talents.

Watercolour by Percy French

The Old Museum Building, Trinity College Dublin, the Engineering School in Percy French's time.

Image reproduced courtesy of the Engineering School whose offices and this painting still remain in the building.

7. AN EARLY LITERARY CONTRIBUTION

J.L. Toole, 'a celebrated comic actor'

What Percy French describes in later years as his 'only contribution to contemporary literature' during his time in college was a ballad called 'Abdallah Bulbul Ameer'. This was composed to be part of his repertoire for college smoking concerts, which were a fashionable part of university life in those days (presumably it was unnecessary for everyone to smoke). Written in 1877, when in his mid-twenties, this was a rather sophisticated but inevitably humorous reflection on the war then in progress mainly between the Russian and the Ottoman empires. The ballad told of two cleverly conceived, if maybe stereotypical, characters in a duel: the brave Abdallah Bulbul Ameer, of whom 'none were so reckless of life or of limb' and the equally brave, heroic and enviably talented Russian, Ivan Potschjinski Skidar, who could 'imitate Toole, play eucher and pool and perform on the Spanish guitar.' The somewhat truculent Abdallah Bulbul provokes an altercation by accusing the Russian of 'standing on his toe' whilst his reference to his opponent as 'infidel' is suggestive of the religious background underlying the real war.

As will be seen as usual with Percy French, a serious background event is given comic and clever interpretation; he is well informed not just on the international scene but also on the more local theatrical activity. 'Toole' mentioned in the ballad was J.L. Toole who, according to James N. Healy's book *Percy French and his Songs* was a celebrated comic actor of the time. In the 1877-8 war Russia was declared the victor, but in French's 'comic song' both protagonists die in a fight to the end. This is perhaps a moral or analogy for both the lack of real victors in the long-running Russo–Turkish antipathy and also for the outcome of wars in general. However good the ballad was (and is) as light entertainment, it could only have been composed by an observant, incisive, broadly educated and youthful mind. According to French's sister, the song was amusingly dedicated to the Turkish military hero Osman Pascha, as supposedly sung by him in the Shipka Pass. After the Turkish War Osman Pascha's nephew arrived in Dublin to study the working of the Royal Irish Constabulary. He came across French's song and sent a copy to his uncle!

Like much of Percy French's later work, the song should be delivered slowly, with a knowing style, facial expression and appropriate emphases. Young W. French had also to compose suitable music for his ballad and as is more often than not the case, successful song writing is a combination of lyric and tune. Brendan O'Dowda, one of the finest voices to interpret Percy French's songs, described the air as both 'undignified and unforgettable'. Maybe it was for both reasons that the song became so popular at the college smoking concerts that he decided to publish it. He borrowed £5 from 'Archie' West (did he ever pay it back?) and recounts that, 'when Cranmer & Co. handed me 200 copies to be disposed of at one and sixpence a copy, Eldorado seemed round the corner'. Sadly, French neglected to take out copyright, a London firm brought out a pirated edition and he was tricked out of all rights to his song. The pirated edition (called 'Abdul Abulbul Ameer') included minor changes (not for the better) and its rhythmic air went all over the English-speaking world as a popular ditty. Most of the singers and whistlers knew or cared little of its 'literary' origins.

American singer and composer Frank Crumit (1889–1943) will forever be associated with Percy French because he made the pirated version of 'Abdallah Bulbul Ameer' (i.e. 'Abdul Abulbul Ameer') virtually his own. Frank, 'an adept ukulele player' and prolific songwriter, was as it happened also an engineer in his early life. His repertoire included comic songs, minstrel songs and ballads but 'without any doubt', according to a biographical sketch by one Kevin Daly, 'Frank's most popular song was Abdul Abulbul Amir [sic] written by Irish composer Percy French'.

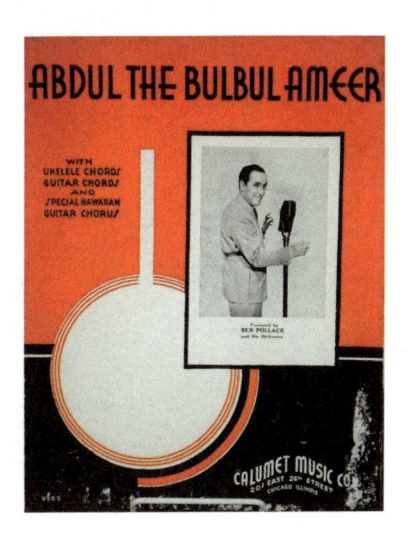

Song cover 'Abdul the Bulbul Ameer'

In the 1985 summer edition of *This England*, the following letter appeared:

> Sir, In the 1920s with a few other juniors of the United States Army, I was stationed in Paris on duties related to the War Memorials of World War I. Occasionally, with our families, we would get together for dinner followed by a singsong. In 1929 we were joined by a youngish major who taught us the words of 'Abdul Abulbul Ameer'. He sang it well. His name? Dwight D. Eisenhower, of whom we learnt much more later! – signed: Thomas North, Maj. General U.S. Army (Ret.) Washington D.C.

Brendan O'Dowda quotes from another source: 'it has sounded in the Australian outbacks, the diamond mines of South Africa, on the cattle trails of the West and on the decks of Arctic trawlers', without, of course, royalty to its composer. Happily, however, almost a century later Brendan was successful in persuading the guilty publishers to belatedly enrol W. French as the undisputed author.

Frank Crumit (1889-1943) and Julia Sanderson

'A radio team'

Percy French Society Archives

8. 'THE WORLD AND WE WERE IN OUR PRIME ONCE, ONLY ONCE, UPON A TIME'

From the poem 'Not lost but gone before'
by Percy French

Mrs De Burgh Daly refers to the 'terrible years of the 1880s', meaning the anti-landlord political agitation of that time, but there is little record of it interfering with her brother's carefree lifestyle. Armed at last in 1881 with his C.E. degree, W. French initially found that there was no rush for his services from the giants of the industrial revolution ('none of them seemed able to find my address'). Indeed the industrial revolution reaching its peak in Britain and to an extent in the northeast of Ireland must have seemed light years away from Cloonyquin, Cavan and their environs. There is evidence in a Foyle and Londonderry College Past Pupils Magazine that 'W. French, B.A., C.E.' spent some time back at Foyle College as a temporary teacher of art. He marked this short time by presenting watercolours of the school to the headmaster's wife, Mrs Hime.

He did commence an engineering career, albeit in a rather low-key way. He 'put in the time' for a while as an apprentice under one James Price, Engineer-in-Chief of the Midland Railway (the M.G.W.R.). This short period, when there was little work to do, was distinguished by his teaming up with fellow apprentice Charles Manners (then known as Charles Mansergh), the future famous opera singer. With French on banjo and Manners providing bones accompaniment they blackened their faces and spent a day entertaining both the 'crowd' and the 'carriage folk' at Punchestown Races. Neither group, it seems, was impressed. According to the unreliable memory of W. French they made only eight pence between them but Manners, less inclined to exaggerate, remembered a more successful outing both artistically (he hoped) and financially (28 shillings). Both Manners and French, as it happened, were destined to make their careers in the musical and entertainment worlds.

It was not just the victims of famine and land clearance who faced the emigrant ship. W. French, B.A., C.E. had his bags (portmanteau, in his words) packed for Manitoba in Canada when unexpectedly he was appointed by the Irish Board of Works to be Inspector of Loans to Tenants under a government drainage scheme for County Cavan. His professional work was to ensure the drains were properly planned and made before expectant farmers availed themselves of the government loans. Although this was somewhat removed from the furnace driven mills of the industrial revolution, he was a little further along the road towards fulfilling his father's dream. Not that he was likely to be anyway pretentious about his success. A.D. Godley, his friend and contributor to the home-produced magazine, 'The Trombone of Truth', notes his reprieve from the emigrant ship in humorous verse:

> *We heard with much regret that you*
> *The Western shores were going to,*
> *But now it seems you are to have an*
> *Appointment on the 'sewers' of Cavan.*

'Sewers' was pronounced 'shores' in the west. A.D. Godley was to become Public Orator of Oxford and Dean of Magdalen College.

In return, W. French, C.E., with his ever-ready pen and sense of the mock-heroic, was inspired to write the famous 'The Effusion of William, Inspector of Drains':

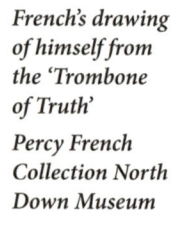

French's drawing of himself from the 'Trombone of Truth'

Percy French Collection North Down Museum

Let others betake them to Western plains,
And ease the redman of his ill-gotten gains,
No tomahawk ever shall enter the brains
Of William, the local Inspector of Drains.

He mounts his tall trap, gives his charger the reins,
And gallops away through the green country lanes,
The board pays the posting – the balance remains
With William, the local Inspector of Drains.

He finds out the holding and what it contains,
Then marks out his system in furlongs and chains
And points out positions for 'minors' and 'mains' –
Such wisdom has William, Inspector of Drains.

He plunges through marshes long haunted by cranes,
Quite heedless of how the dark bog-water stains;
Traducers assert that this ardour he feigns:
They little know William, Inspector of Drains.

He stays in his quarters, of course, if it rains,
And wakes the piano's voluptuous strains
And if of delay the bold tenant complains,
He's sat on by William, Inspector of Drains.

The fair maids of Cavan (this William maintains),
Tho' I think one should take it with salt, a few grains,
Have left in a body their woe-begone swains
For William, the local Inspector of Drains!

'Tis an honorous post – but the writer refrains
From dwelling at length on its pleasures and pains,
It may not last long, but as yet he remains
Yours faithfully, William, Inspector of Drains.

Godley mischievously sent these verses to French's boss, Mr Le Fanu, the Commissioner of Public Works, with a note in verse:

> *This copy of verses, the writer explains,*
> *Must be sent back forthwith under heaviest pains.*
> *Although the receiver might plead that he reigns*
> *Supreme over all the Inspectors of Drains.*

Mr Le Fanu writes in reply:

> *With thanks he returns (but a copy retains)*
> *The verses, whose cleverness clearly contains*
> *Proof positive what a large quantum of brains*
> *Has William the local Inspector of Drains.*

But not before the Assistant Commissioner adds:

> *The Assistant Commissioner copies these strains,*
> *Is officially angry, but kindly refrains*
> *From expressing more strongly the manner it pains*
> *Him to learn how the time of Inspector of Drains*
> *Is spent with fair maids in the green Cavan lanes,*
> *While the Assistant Commissioner thinks that their brains,*
> *Are engaged night and day in reporting on drains,*
> *To the Assistant Commissioner nothing remains*
> *But to state with what pleasure he always maintains*
> *That, although there may be on their coats a few stains*
> *There are none on the names of Inspector of Drains.*

And then the Assistant Commissioner's daughter adds a slightly caustic female perspective:

> *The Assistant Commissioner's daughter maintains*
> *That Inspectors who dawdle indoors when it rains*
> *Making impartial love to the Betsys and Janes*
> *Are not worthy to rank as Inspectors of Drains.*
>
> *She thinks it most doubtful a redman would deign*
> *To blunt a new tomahawk over the brain*
> *Or rather the place where it ought to have lain*
> *Of a person whose intellect's spent in a drain.*

However, the Commissioner puts a constructive and learned slant on matters:

> *One hint I would venture before the thing wanes,*
> *That our Chairman should see these most exquisite strains,*
> *Little thinks he what fancy could shoot from the brains*
> *Of one who descends to the depths of the Drains.*
> *De profundis clamavi! but no one disdains*
> *What the pen of the poet so clearly explains,*
> *And a Cynic is he who objects or complains*
> *Of the idylls of William, Inspector of Drains.*

French's time in Cavan as Inspector of Drains was indeed destined to be idyllic. *Chronicles* written in later life reflect a sense of well-being and a light-hearted attitude to living: 'Three hundred pounds a year and travelling expenses was untold wealth to a bachelor boy with my simple wants, so having bought a new set of banjo strings and a tennis racquet, I set off to take up my duties.' These duties were not too daunting. He was able, he records, to withstand any attempts at bribery because of such a wealth-producing salary. The very idea of a government loan usually brings out the least attractive characteristics of the population; the house in Cavan town where he stayed with the devoted Mrs Cole was often on market day besieged by farmers with requests for the Inspector to examine potential drainage improvements on their farms. His housekeeper fended them off by stretching the truth a little in saying he was already on his rounds!

Photo courtesy of Cavan County Museum

W. French, C.E. had notable difficulty with a clergyman whose demand for a loan for a cattle shed was in reality to be spent on a billiard room and conservatory. There was no mention at all of digging a drain and the applicant was not at all pleased when he was told by the Inspector that it was impossible to teach a cow to play billiards or to take an interest in orchids. It all suggests his parody of the sad poem 'Alone (after Sw-nb-ne)':

> *Oh house with the tumble-down gable,*
> *Oh water ways wealthy with weeds,*
> *Oh holding devoid of a stable,*
> *Oh rushes and reeds*
> *How long will ye view with contrition*
> *Your lands lie unlaboured and unsown,*
> *Nor seek for that kindly magician*
> *A Government Loan?*

Having remembered to pack his banjo at the outset and found kindred musical souls in Cavan, there soon emerged The Kinnypottle Komics, a Christy's Minstrel group named after the Kinneypottle stream that wends its way (nowadays mostly under ground) through Cavan town. The special talents of W. French, C.E. would also be welcomed in the local musical and dramatic society. The printed programme for a triple bill show by the society on 11 March 1887 shows the production of a comic operetta *A Simple Sweep*, the 'latest London success' with the title role undertaken by 'Mr W. French'. Playing opposite him was 'pretty Mary Kennedy' ('Daddy had a flirtation with her once', his daughter Ettie would later comment). After the interval came a 'Topical Duet' given by 'French & Radcliffe' which was followed by *Naval Engagements*, a comedy in two acts. This time it was 'Mr W. Percy French' who was in action as a naval officer, an occasion when he begins to use his second name in more formal-type situations. *The Cavan Weekly News* gave a special mention to the drop curtain decorated with 'French' cartoons and a jumble of witty non sequiturs from half covered advertisements: 'Mothers are you troubled in your rest by – Our waterproof boots worn by all the leading – Cockroaches?'

The Kinnypottle Komics poster

Percy French Society Archives

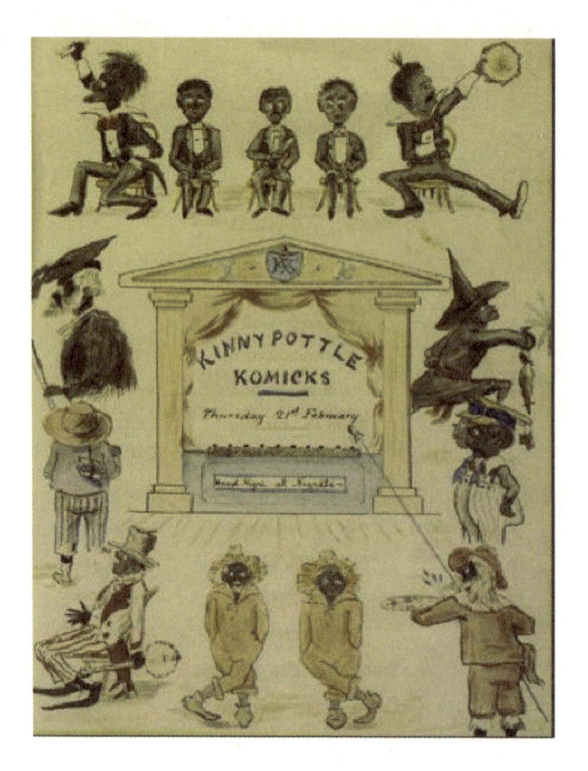

This was a time when an older social order still prevailed and the locally named 'Protestant Hall' (still extant in the 1980s) would then have been the centre of social and cultural activity. The better-off landlord and professional classes still enjoyed a more privileged lifestyle, mixing together at the tennis club or in the musical and dramatic society. One of W. French's closest friends from those Cavan days was the Bank of Ireland manager J.W. Weekes, who recalled them using the cycling fashions of the time (himself on a fifty-six-inch-high penny-farthing and W.F. on a 'Kangaroo') to visit mutual friends the Rotherhams in Crossdrum. Apparently there were two roads to Crossdrum and as sometimes drainage schemes were underway on each route, W. French, C.E. would inspect one farm and Mr Weekes, the other; 'by this means another day off for tennis was secured.'

> *Then the day I went a-wheeling,*
> *Round the lovely shores of Sheelin,*
> *When the perfume of the Primrose told that spring had really come,*
> *And I rode my cycle dreaming*
> *That Beauty's eyes were beaming,*
> *And I'd find céad míle fáilte in the halls of old Crossdrum!*
>
> A verse from 'Red Letter Days' c.1908

W. French, C.E. needed as many days off as possible, not just for playing tennis, but also for writing about it and writing on the subject of cycling as well. He was by now a regular contributor to *The Irish Cyclist and Athlete*, which was thriving with the growing enthusiasm for cycling as a sport and recreation. At some point the local 'Inspector of Drains' used a then very up-to-date but ultimately short-lived tricycle, with the brand name Excelsior, as an alternative to the outside car for visiting farms on his professional rounds. His daughter Ettie, in her memoir *Willie*, maintained that this was an economy measure so that he could save his travelling expenses for other purposes. This indeed appears to be so and there were all kinds of 'other purposes'. But, despite problems with hills and rough roads, there was also no doubting an initial delight in the riding of the tricycle as expressed in his parody of Henry Wadsworth Longfellow's epic poem of which the first verse reads:

> *The shades of night were falling fast,*
> *As through an Alpine village passed*
> *A youth, who bore, 'mid snow and ice,*
> *A banner with the strange device,*
> *'Excelsior!'*

The W. French, C.E. version:

> *The shades of night had almost fled*
> *As through a Cavan village sped*
> *A youth who bore upon his tric-*
> *Ycle this somewhat strange device,*
> *'Excelsior!'*

Having courageously (one would expect) resisted the entreaties of a maiden fair 'to stay and rest', the real motive for his late night adventure emerges in the final verse:

> *Methinks it was the greed of gain*
> *Which urged him thus across the plain.*
> *No rest thy wheels may know the while*
> *They pay him eighteen pence per mile*
> *'Excelsior!'*

During these busy and creative years of the mid 1880s W. French, C.E. with the pen name Will Wagtale began to contribute articles to *The Irish Cyclist and Athlete* magazine. A friendly relationship was growing between the 'Inspector of Drains' and R.J. Mecredy, the great Irish cycling champion who edited, owned and published the magazine. Taking time away from his primary duties W. French was a regular partaker in cycling tours to places of scenic interest such as Glendalough, Killarney and ultimately to Scotland, when his sense of fun would be invaluable around the campfires. His involvement with R.J. Mecredy would, as it happens, prove fateful in the years to come.

French's drawings from the 'Trombone of Truth'
Percy French Collection North Down Museum

Photo 'The Killarney Tour'
Percy French Collection North Down Museum

The Irish Cyclist of 15 August 1884 gives Mecredy's account of a Glendalough outing:

> Tea over, Mrs Mecredy and the Rev. Mr Whelan took their departure homewards, while others kept dropping in from town, until over thirty were in camp. An enormous campfire had been lighted in a sheltered hollow, within a few yards of the 'dining saloon' and round it, as darkness fell, the entire party gathered, wrapped in overcoats and rugs. W.P. French was there with his banjo, and Riordan (of Charleville), Harding and Warke (of Derry), and others poured forth song after song.

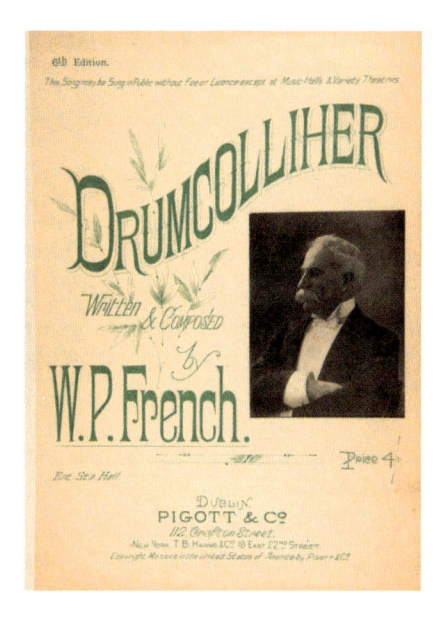

Song cover 'Drumcolliher'

Percy French Collection North Down Museum

It was through his friendship with T.J. Riordan that French came to stay at McAuliffe's all-purpose shop in Drumcolliher, an experience immortalized much later in one of his best-loved songs of that name.

W. French, C.E. was already a lawn tennis enthusiast from his College days; after all with a sense of farsightedness and a degree of strategic planning he had bought a new racquet in preparation for life as a civil engineer. In Cavan there was a tennis court at the home of Lord Farnham and tennis parties were given by enthusiastic folk such as Dr and Mrs Mease. A photograph of the time shows that white tennis dress was not

Tennis party, Cavan

Percy French Collection North Down Museum

yet *de rigueur* even amongst the county types of Cavan. W. French, C.E., on the extreme right in a rare early photograph, looks somewhat laid-back, shy or self-effacing. This recalls a description of him by Sir John Ross, a friend from both French's Foyle College and Trinity College Dublin days, who writing in *Chronicles* remembered him as 'generally in the midst of the gaiety and the life and soul of it all but always looking as solemn as a judge'.

It has been established that W. French, C.E. – who won prizes at the game whilst in Cavan – was to a large extent instrumental in the laying of the tennis courts at the rear of the aforementioned Protestant Hall. In the publication *The History of Irish Tennis* the author, Tom Higgins, notes how French combined his engineering skills with his love of the game in the laying of the courts for which he had many tons of sand transported to Cavan from the beach at Bundoran. But his enthusiastic involvement in the game of lawn tennis was not merely as a player, one who according to Weekes played 'a very nippy game and had a low cut shot which was not easy to return'; there is also much evidence in his writings that it is a game he really enjoyed.

Strangely this interest may also have involved the Buxton Lawn Tennis Club in Derbyshire, a county where the French family appear to have had a residence or family connection. It is mentioned at one point that they 'emigrated' to Derbyshire for educational purposes. In the 1880s Buxton Lawn Tennis Club hosted major tournaments including the All-England Ladies Doubles Championship. In 1884 and 1885 French wrote accounts of the tournaments in verse with admirable illustrations by his friend Walter Pigot, who combined his Irish Land Commission job with a contrasting role as one of French's colleagues in The Kinnypottle Komics in Cavan. 'But now the poet has been sent / To hymn the Buxton Tournament.' The twelve-page 1885 edition, entitled 'White Lines – a Tennis Court Chronicle' was in copperplate script and professionally published to be sold for sixpence per copy. Interestingly, according to the Buxton Club's modern-day web site, the written history of the club uses the identical title, 'White Lines – a Tennis Court Chronicle.'

French reading 'White Lines'
Percy French Collection North Down Museum

9. HIS 'RAY OF SUNSHINE'

*'Then you'll meet the radiant vision who is all the world to you
(You'll attend her mother's lectures later on)'*

From the poem 'Later On' by Percy French

The year of the arrival in Cavan of W. French, C.E. as Inspector of Loans to Tenants ('Inspector of Drains') was 1883 (not 1881 as stated on the blue plaque nowadays denoting the house in Farnham St where he lodged with Mrs Cole). It coincided with the far away earth-shattering volcanic eruption of Krakatoa, an island off the coast of Java (nowadays Indonesia). This might have seemed of little if any import in the rural tranquillity in which the 'Inspector of Drains' was now immersed. But by the late 1880s, volcanic dust being blown across the upper atmosphere from the huge explosion brought spectacular sunsets and colourful hues to the skies over nearby Lough Sheelin. This was a new inspiration for W. French the watercolourist, who according to his friend J.W. Weekes, often painted just the sunsets. Weekes believed that the foundation of W. French's subsequent success as a watercolour artist was laid in Cavan where he also started a sketching club.

'Spectacular Sunset'

Watercolour by Percy French

Percy French Collection North Down Museum

Another friend from that era, W. Harkness, recounted how at the time French, having seen an exhibition of watercolours in Dublin, thought he himself could draw just as well and sent six sketches to the next exhibition – winning five prizes! Shortly afterwards he was exhibiting his watercolours in Dublin and, according to his daughter Ettie, painting eventually became the art he loved most of all. It was the happiest expression of the happiest period of his life

Mrs De Burgh Daly, the excellent editor of *Chronicles and Poems*, appears to have been French's closest sibling and she occasionally accompanied her brother on the outside car (sidecar) when he was doing his drainage inspection work. 'Sometimes', she remembered, 'he sketched, sometimes hummed over airs likely to "go well" to verses he had just composed, or insisted on my singing the melody while he arranged the harmonies'. They often dined or stayed at hospitable country houses where it is most likely that the 'Inspector of Drains' first met the youthful Ethel Armytage Moore, daughter of Hugh Armytage Moore, who was land agent for Lord Farnham.

Ethel Armytage Moore (Ettie)

Percy French Collection North Down Museum

They were living at Arnmore, which is today the clubhouse of Cavan Golf Club. Ethel (Ettie) Armytage Moore was herself a talented artist. Tennis parties and their enthusiasm for watercolour painting would have been additional factors in their growing relationship. French family sources believe Ethel Armytage Moore to have been 'strikingly attractive in an unusual way'. Her colouring was especially wonderful, her sense of fun and lack of airs and graces were her greatest charms. All of these qualities must surely have captivated W. French, C.E. both as an artist and as one by nature more given to fun than conformity.

It cannot be proven conclusively, but many of those who are interested in the story of his life have little difficulty believing that the life-changing coming together of W. French, C.E. and Ethel Armytage Moore (Ettie, his 'ray of sunshine') is reflected in the poem 'On the Road to Ballybay'.

The actual road to Ballybay leading out of Cavan is in this case rather more than a line on a map; it is also symbolic of the meeting of young lovers and the notion of a future walking together through life's ups and downs.

'Peat Bog'
Watercolour by Percy French
Percy French Collection North Down Museum

'Is this the road to Ballybay?'
Sez I to Miss Magee;
'You're leavin' it behind you,'
Sez Maryanne to me.

So I turned and walked beside her,
And 'tis only fair to say
It was very pleasant walkin'
On the road to Ballybay.

Ballybay, Ballybay,
'Twas a dark and winthry day,
But the sun was surely shinin'
On the road to Ballybay.

'Is this the road to fame and wealth?'
Sez I to Miss Magee;
'Ye've got the brains, ye've got the health,'.
Sez Maryanne to me.

'But still I want a comrade
To praise me an' to blame,
An' keep me from the traps that's laid
Upon the road to fame.'

Ballybay, Ballybay,
No man could go asthray
With a guide like her beside him
On the road to Ballybay.

'Is this the road to paradise?'
Sez I to Miss Magee;
'I'm thinking that it might be,'
Sez Maryanne to me;

Oh I saw the love light leppin'
In a pair of roguish eyes
And I knew we two were steppin'
On the road to paradise.

Ballybay, Ballybay,
The birds are far away
But our hearts they sang together
On the road to Ballybay.

Ethel's mother was, however, not enamoured of her daughter's engagement to, by her standards, a penniless engineer. Another daughter Priscilla had married Lord Annesley in Co. Down. If the three hundred pounds a year plus travelling expenses earned by the Inspector of Loans to Tenants cut no ice, neither did his rather popular musical successes like the song 'Phil the Fluter's Ball' or playing a leading role in The Kinnypottle Komics. Nonetheless the couple stuck to their engagement, a tribute perhaps to Ethel's 'strength of character', which was just beginning to be tested. On 28 July 1888 the Board of Works informed W. French, Esq., C.E. that his services would be dispensed with from 30 September owing to the 'marked decrease' in the number of loans being applied for under the relevant Land Act. Worse still, a distillery in which he had invested his savings failed completely. It was rather ironic that his aversion to alcohol had not influenced his investment strategy!

At this major turning point in the life of William Percy French we already note a hugely prolific output of writings. This included a number of successful songs, all of which were accomplished while French was fully involved in the immediate social, cultural and indeed engineering activities of Cavan. It required time and organisation to get to Dublin or Buxton in Derbyshire. This was over a relatively short five-year period.

Overall we are aware of a private and sensitive person, with much creative talent, a playboy in style and one who is the life and soul of whatever group activity in which he may be involved. At the same time, he is rather reserved and unwilling to place himself to the forefront of social events or groupings. Perhaps his old tutor the Rev. James Rountree remembered him well, 'He could be grave and gay, humorous or pathetic, but his style was always delicate and restrained. Never any coarseness or exaggeration.'

10. SONGS FROM THE 1880s

One of the earlier songs linked with W. French was composed in association with John Ross, his friend from student days. Sir John's future career as Chancellor of Ireland took a more establishment-based, if less renowned, place in the annals of Ireland than that of his co-author of 'Andy McElroe', an amusing song about a soldier set against the background of the mid-1880s warfare in the Anglo-Egyptian Sudan. Again there is an anti-heroic quality, humorously portrayed, in the story of 'Brave Andy McElroe', whose letters from the desert tended to be somewhat at variance with reality. To quote Sir John: 'To hear French render one of these (comic) songs with a perfectly solemn face was a thing one could never forget.'

Songs subsequently published by W.P. French, written mainly during his 'engineering' years in Co. Cavan, include 'A Man by the Name of Maguire', 'Cornelius Burke' and the more famous duo of 'Phil the Fluter's Ball' and 'Slattery's Mounted Fut'. The composer's brief account (in *Chronicles*) of the event that inspired 'Phil the Fluter's Ball' is itself a joy to read. In case the passing years might have embellished his description of the episode, the essence of it is that the Rev. James Godley, Rector of Drominchin near Carrigallen in Co. Leitrim, whilst enjoying a walk encountered Phil, a neighbouring smallholder who had defrayed his rent arrears by giving a ball in his home.

The rather grand idea of a 'ball' in a cabin no doubt excited the imaginations of both the Rev. Godley and W.P. French, although Phil's idea was not that far removed from the subscription concerts that social historian Edward Royle explains, 'were the means by which gentlemen financed their leisure' in earlier years. Anyway, with food and drink locked safely away and a cap left, as the song recounts – 'convaniant to the dure' where 'the more they put in the better would the music be for batterin' the flure' – the resultant song is descriptive of an occasion of pure uninhibited gaiety.

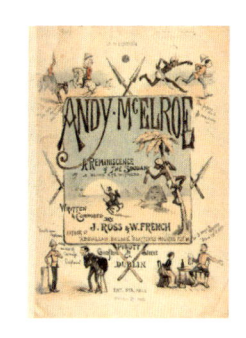

Song cover 'Andy McElroe'
Percy French Collection North Down Museum

Song cover 'Phil the Fluter's Ball'
Percy French Collection North Down Museum

Gaiety Theatre programme
Percy French Collection North Down Museum

The participating guests are beautifully characterized: the energetic Widda' Cafferty who was 'leppin' like a hare' and 'little crooked Paddy' who was also able to play a part (he passed the caubeen round). The 'beautiful Miss Bradys', whose hotelier family in real life had a pony and trap for hire, might have felt slightly demeaned to be relegated to a less up-market 'private ass and cart', nonetheless, their acknowledged beauty was not forgotten.

The world premiere of 'Phil the Fluter's Ball' quite appropriately took place in Carrigallen with a first public performance by its composer at the local schoolhouse. French was taken to the event by sidecar driven by jarvey George Rosemond, who maintained that the real premiere of the song was aboard his sidecar with an audience of himself and his horse Neddy! The song has since travelled far and wide but mainly in memory of that historic occasion, the Old Bredagh Schoolhouse in Carrigallen was excellently restored for church and community purposes in 2013.

Over the years, 'Phil the Fluter's Ball' was often used as the foundation or framework for musical productions from London to Bangor, Co. Down. The February 1991 issue of *The Amateur Stage* reported on a show *Phil the Fluter* by the Portsmouth Players which 'packed the Kings Theatre'. It was a musical loosely based on the story of the early life of Percy French. It was, most probably, the original *Golden Years* musical that had been staged at many Irish theatres throughout the 1960s before changing its title to *Phil the Fluter* for London's Palace Theatre in 1969 or 70, when it starred Stanley Baxter, Evelyn Laye and former 'pop star' turned actor Mark Wynter. 'Phil the Fluter's Ball' was also a choreographed scene in Patricia Mulholland's *Irish Folk Ballet*, which flourished in Belfast towards the second half of the twentieth century.

Brendan O'Dowda in *The World of Percy French* tells of a priest named Father P.J. O'Brien who was domiciled in Lusaka, Zambia. He loved the songs of Percy French and was instrumental in translating the chorus and three verses of 'Phil the Fluter's Ball' into Latin. Latin was apparently the only language understood by all the multinational members of the Church and legal fraternity in the Lusaka of the time.

The background inspiration to another major success, 'Slattery's Mounted Fut', is unclear but may have something to do with rumours of private armies or maybe other underground activity at the time.

'Slattery's Mounted Fut' is set mockingly in the context of such historic figures as Julius Caesar and Napoleon and an unlikely overcoming of the Turks by the Cork Militia at Waterloo. An anti-heroic and anti-war feeling is engendered in an outrageous send up of an imaginary private army, one however that is still not bereft of the human elements of courage, weakness and respect for the law (well, up to a point). The excuse for a probably sensible withdrawal is finally uttered by Slattery: 'Best be a coward for five minutes than a dead man all your life.' Charles U. Daly of Boston, grandson of Mrs De Burgh Daly referred to this line with darkish humour at a reunion dinner of United States Marines in 2014.

Song cover 'Slattery's Mounted Fut'

Percy French Collection North Down Museum

More unusually, in the context of French's lifestyle at the time, the song 'The Emigrant Ship' is full of the pain and sadness associated with emigration as experienced in nineteenth-century Ireland. Its plaintive melody combined with lines such as 'Why on my cheek the tear of bitterness?' is in the form of the Victorian ballad, usually sung with gravitas around the piano in the drawing rooms of the upper classes. It demonstrates a depth of feeling that takes French's songwriting outside the purely comic classification.

Also with these songs we can begin to perceive the ear of French for the local idiom, a most important part of his literary legacy. The late and learned Derek Collie, from the town of Ballymena, was renowned for his knowledge of the local geography, topography, social history and culture of all of Ireland. Mention any townland or village in any part of the island and Derek could immediately reveal the most detailed knowledge of its landscape, people and language. To quote Derek: 'Percy French had an acute ear for the local idiom, – an ability not given to all great poets – patterns of speech and thought revealing the character and expression of the people.'

French performing 'Carmody's Mare'

Percy French Collection North Down Museum

Derek compared Percy French to the great English novelist George Eliot and also to Ireland's famed satirist Myles na gCopaleen. This somewhat undervalued legacy of French would be further emphasised by him in later years in his short plays such as 'Michael O'Ryan Gets the Pension' and also savoured in his famous monologue 'Carmody's Mare'. The latter, like his rhythmic song 'Sweet Marie', is so evocative of the excitement of point-to-point racing in Ireland a century ago. In *The Irish Book Lover* of March 1921, after French's death, Canon Hannay (aka novelist George A. Birmingham) wrote: 'The genius of Percy French as entertainer, artist and author was a national asset, and the fact that his words and phrases had become family bywords was a mark of real greatness.'

11. THE 'JARVEY' YEARS

Oh, my optimistic hero, there are lessons you must learn
In the queer time that is coming later on;
And masters and examiners you'll find at every turn,
In the hard times that are coming later on.

From the poem 'Later On' by Percy French

With his services as Inspector of Loans to Tenants in Co. Cavan no longer required, W. French, who had been contributing 'humorous prose and verse' to *The Irish Cyclist and Athlete*, approached the editor R.J. Mecredy for a permanent post. In French's own words Mecredy 'told me he would do better than that, he would make me editor of a brand new weekly comic paper to be called *The Jarvey*. This opportunity surely provided the ideal outlet for French's by now very evident abilities to write with a light touch and to ameliorate the more controversial aspects of life with satirical humour. It would also be a source of badly needed regular income; he was of course engaged to be married to Ethel Armytage Moore.

Image of the front cover of the first issue of The Jarvey

Artist, Richard C. Orpen, R.H.A.

Percy French Collection North Down Museum

The 'Jarvey' Years

The first issue of *The Jarvey* appeared on the bookstands on 3 January 1889. The artist Richard C. Orpen, one of French's great friends from student days, elaborately illustrated the front cover. It featured in the centre a drawing of a genial, cape-attired jarvey giving a welcoming flick of his finger. Orpen also provided most of the internal cartoons in this inaugural issue. The title of the publication was no doubt inspired by the reputation of the drivers of horse drawn hackney sidecars (jaunting cars) who were, like modern taxi drivers, often the source of comment, rumour and anecdote. The back cover consisted of advertisements for various products, including the numerous publications of Mecredy & Kyle and interestingly, 'Three new comic songs by W. P. French – Andy McElroe, Slattery's Mounted Fut and Phil the Fluter's Ball'. The editor's name is given in the style of 'Mr W.P. French.' French's editorial introduction provides something akin to the journal's policy; in typical fashion it is a verse addressed to one Brian Magee and it is clear that the intention is 'comic', with political groups and other 'factions' to be ignored:

> 'I mean that the sheet will be comic –
> We're humorous people, they say,
> Though lately we've been economic
> In anything tending that way;
> But now, the bad times are gone bye, sir,
> An' trade's on the mend, d'ye see,
> Though that may be only a lie, sir.'
> 'You're right, sir,' said Mr Magee
>
> 'With regard now to politics, Brian,
> One cannot to both parties tend;
> It's hard and it's no use denyin',
> To keep from offendin' a friend.
> You cannot well run with the hounds, sir,
> And coorse with the hare, d'ye see;
> Both parties would think you unsound, sir.'
> 'You're right sir,' said Mr Magee.

'Truth from The Well'

Drawing by Richard C. Orpen, R.H.A.

Percy French Collection North Down Museum

The resultant sixteen-page weekly magazine was attractively and artistically laid out. It might be described as sophisticated, urbane, sometimes witty and clever, occasionally a little obscure or naive and certainly not in the nature of populist readership. A review of the first issue by Jakes McCarthy of the powerful *Freeman's Journal* did not help: 'We have before us the first number of a journal devoted to art and humour. Some of the jokes we've seen before – some we haven't seen yet.'

And, having put this first issue together with much imagination and creative effort, the editor would very soon have been faced with the daunting prospect of having to repeat the process within a seven day cycle into the future. One feels that, at least, a small team of talented writers and illustrators would have been necessary to keep such a major project underway. However, as French subsequently recorded, 'We started with no capital whatsoever, and the idea was to pay the artists and writers out of the profits of the first month. At the end of the first month there were no profits, at the end of the second month there were no writers or artists except my very good friends, Dick Orpen and Eddy Radcliffe.' It was perhaps surprising that R.J. Mecredy, who promoted the idea and who was himself an established publisher, did not ensure that sufficient capital was invested to maintain standards while a viable readership grew and became established. The history of similar Dublin comic journals was not good and another big challenge was to overcome the market stranglehold of similar style English productions.

Notwithstanding such rather permanent 'teething problems', there also emerged The Jarvey Concert Company as a kind of spin-off from the journalistic efforts of French and his friend Radcliffe. Heavily advertised (without cost?) in *The Jarvey* itself, this 'Grand Series of Concerts' was performed initially in major halls and theatres around Dublin (Rotunda, Dalkey etc.) and then travelled all over Ireland from Cork to Belfast and Coleraine. Its second Annual Tour in April 1890 took in Oldcastle, Cavan, Clones, Enniskillen, Omagh and Dungannon. A fascinating programme consisted of 'The Banjo Band', 'Professor Leozedgt (the Marvellous Prestidigitateur)', 'The Lightning Limmer' and 'Humorous Songs and Stories by Messers French and Radcliffe.' It is not unlikely that French himself was involved in most of these entertainment acts! Anyway, press reviews were universally positive. Such success may have rewarded the promoters individually for their unselfish journalistic endeavours or, at least, may have helped underpin the flimsy financial state of *The Jarvey* itself.

However, with what must have been extraordinary application and creative energy from the editor and his friends and despite such imaginative and worthy distractions as The Jarvey Concert Company, *The Jarvey* itself kept going. It was of course of vital importance to French, then aged thirty-six and engaged to be married, that the project should succeed. Soon his fiancée, Ethel (Ettie) Armytage Moore (shortly to be Mrs E.K. French) – herself an excellent artist and illustrator – helped him in his efforts.

'The Mill'

Drawing by Mrs E.K. French for The Jarvey

Percy French Collection North Down Museum

Sometimes, French related, when he found himself 'three or four columns short' in the make up of an issue, he and Eddy Radcliffe would expand 'paragraphs into stories and couplets into sonnets' while Ettie would search the wastepaper basket for rejected 'love tales' to give to the 'Printer's Devil' waiting for 'a column more'. A clever parody of Edgar Allen Poe's foreboding poem 'The Raven' served the dual purpose of humorously alleviating the unrelenting editorial pressures and at the same time providing a 'column more' for the 'Printer's Devil'.

First verse of 'The Raven' by Edgar Allan Poe:

> *Once upon a midnight dreary, while I pondered weak and weary,*
> *Over many a quaint and curious volume of forgotten lore,*
> *While I nodded, nearly napping, suddenly there came a tapping,*
> *As of some one gently rapping, rapping at my chamber door,*
> *'Tis some visitor,' I muttered, 'rapping at my chamber door –*
> *Only this and nothing more.'*

First verse of 'The Devil' by Percy French:

> *On a winter's evening dreary, as I pondered worn and weary*
> *Over many an ancient chestnut of the dismal days of yore;*
> *Suddenly I heard a tapping, as of some one gently rapping,*
> *And there came a little chap in, who the name of 'Devil' bore,*
> *Who the name of 'Printer's Devil' and the ghastly message bore –*
> *'Foreman wants a column more'.*

'The Devil Awaits'

Drawing by Mrs E.K. French of her husband at work on The Jarvey

Percy French Collection North Down Museum

Occasionally a parody from the 'Trombone of Truth' would be unearthed in the cause. An example is the 'Travellers Hymn', an ode to the Midland Great Western Railway. With uncanny prescience it refers to *Bradshaw's Guide*, made famous in our time by the BBC television series, Great Railway Journeys : 'What news of *Bradshaw's Guide*! (As a rule thou tellest the truth.)'

The Jarvey of 15 March 1890 included a new song, 'The Snakes He Left Behind or St Patrick Up To Date', in which French in his half-serious satirical style shows us his social conscience. The snakes that then needed to be eradicated from Irish society included the maltreatment of children, sweated labour, the 'Serpent of Drink' and a statue of King William in Dublin's College Green, of which:

> *Its proportions are wrong,*
> *For its legs are too long,*
> *And I cannot tell who designed him;*
> *But I'd say, from the look,*
> *That the model he took*
> *Was a reptile the Saint left behind him!*

If French were around today he would find that of those four 'snakes' King William's statue is perhaps the only one that has completely disappeared from 'this beautiful Isle of the Ocean!'

As if the challenge of keeping *The Jarvey* afloat was not enough, during these busy years, Richard Orpen and French, a member of Dublin's Fitzwilliam Lawn Tennis Club, combined to produce artistic and humorous magazines on the subject of tennis, such as *Racquety Rhymes* and *Fitzwilliam Square: A Lawn Tennis Lay*.

The booklet *Racquety Rhymes* cleverly parodies the best-known children's nursery rhymes in order to poke some gentle fun at the idiosyncrasies of the ordinary tennis club members. The 'pot hunter' was a feature of those times no less than today:

> *Bah bah blacklegs, Have you any pots?*
> *'Yes sir, yes sir, lots and lots,*
> *One is a carriage clock; another is a mug*
> *One is a salver and one a claret jug.'*

From Racquety Rhymes

Percy French Collection North Down Museum

Fitzwilliam Square: A Lawn Tennis Lay is a mock eulogy on the larger-than-life heroes of the tennis court and is based on Lord Macaulay's weighty tome *Lays of Ancient Rome*:

> *I myself have played at tennis,*
> *Looked upon myself as fair,*
> *Till I saw the world wide Champions*
> *Battling in Fitzwilliam Square:*
> *Then I saw myself a duffer*
> *Saw that if I longed for fame*
> *I must seek another pastime*
> *I must seek another game ...*
>
> *Many a time I've seen the Renshaws*
> *Rise triumphant from the fray*
> *Like a pair of mighty planets*
> *Shining in the milky way:*
> *Often to the white pavilion*
> *Where the sandwiches they munch*
> *Have I seen the lion Lawford*
> *Sloping slowly to his lunch ...*

Fitzwilliam L.T.C. Championship Meeting 1893

H.F. Lawford with racquet, seated centre

E. Renshaw with racquet, standing centre

Courtesy of Fitzwilliam L.T.C.

Present day tennis aficionados will be interested to know that William Renshaw won the Lawn Tennis Championship of England at Wimbledon on seven successive occasions. His brother Ernest Renshaw and Herbert Lawford were also championship winners of that era. Sometimes the objects of *The Jarvey* and the Fitzwilliam Lawn Tennis Club coincided in, for example, Supplement to *The Jarvey: The Fall of Fitz-illium* a parody on a Homer epic. Much of French's writing on tennis was reproduced in the history of the Fitzwilliam Club, *The Fitzwilliam Story 1877-1977*.

In August 1890 the columns of *The Jarvey* announced the publication of the booklet, 'The First Lord Liftenant and Other Tales', written by French and illustrated by Richard Orpen. It is a hilarious caricature in the Dublin vernacular of the doomed but allegedly once-intimate relationship between Queen Elizabeth I and Lord Essex (her first Lord Lieutenant in Ireland). The 'Other Tales' are similar travesties involving Oliver Cromwell in Rathmines and the wedding of French's old historical 'friend', Strongbow. Although he was editor and had all the responsibility of publishing *The Jarvey* every week, French (as Will Wagtail or Will Wagtale) also continued to be a major contributor to *The Irish Cyclist and Athlete*.

The booklet 'R.J. Mecredy: The Father of Irish Motoring', written by Bob Montgomery, contains Mecredy's account of leaving *The Irish Cyclist* magazine in the editorial hands of Percy French whilst on a cycling tour in 1889: 'On my return I found a sheaf of indignant letters from cyclists who had written asking for advice on various matters, and who complained that they had been insulted and made fools of. It appears that French, who was incapable of answering most of the conundrums put, had turned 'Answers to Correspondents' page into a sort of comic discourse, using the letters received as his text. It amused those who had not asked questions immensely, but the victims failed to see the humour of the situation.'

R.J. Mecredy
Courtesy of
R.I.A.C Archive

Ettie
Mrs E.K. French
Percy French
Collection North
Down Museum

Wm. Percy French and Ethel Kathleen Armytage Moore were married on 28 June 1890 at St Stephen's Church, Dublin. The wedding party, the newspaper announcement stated, was 'confined to the immediate relatives of the bride and groom.' They spent a honeymoon at Castle Howard, Avoca, Co. Wicklow with the Brooke family, who were relatives and friends. 'I had married on the strength of my income as editor, and a happier more hopeful couple cannot be imagined', he later wrote. The newly-weds lived at Victoria Lodge, 3 St John's Road, Sandymount in Dublin and were seen by others as extraordinarily happy together. However, fate had some dark episodes in store. R.J. Mecredy decided that the 1890 Christmas number would be the last issue of *The Jarvey*. As ever, meeting the unwelcome news both positively and with typical humour, French made this last effort a great one. He advertised that original stories and poems by great authors from Chaucer to Conan Doyle would be featured, stories he would write and submit to himself as editor! Yes, in a manner of speaking, *The Jarvey*, in his own words, had 'gone down with colours flying.'

Overall one can only express astonishment that French and friends maintained the comic weekly at such an acceptable standard for an unbroken period of two years. Having eschewed any kind of political comment at a time when such speeches filled the pages of a highly politicized press, it was indeed a brave effort. Later, in his short play *Michael O'Ryan Gets the Pension*, French's long standing disillusionment with the popular press can be deduced from the scene in which Michael is reading aloud a speech about land drainage (of which French had some experience). It was from a speech supposedly given by the local J.P and printed in *The Farmer's Intelligence and Ballyboden Banner of Liberty*: 'Men of Ballyboden! Standing as I do with one foot firmly imbedded in the whirlpool of political agitation, an' the other buried to the hilt in the quagmire of municipal reform, am I to see our noble river torn up by its roots, and its ashes scattered to the four winds of Heaven!'

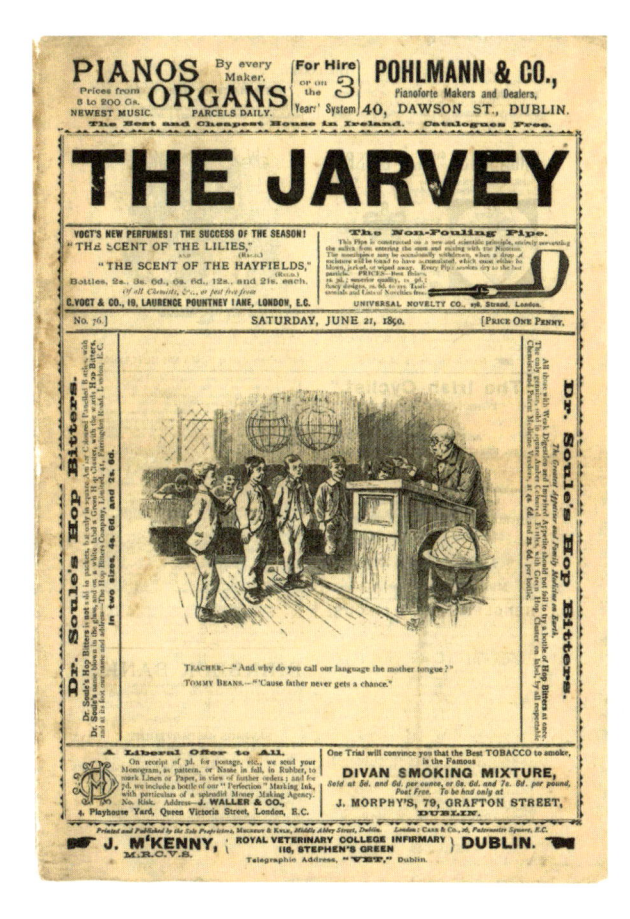

Cover of The Jarvey
Issue 21 June 1890
Percy French Collection
North Down Museum

Note: *The only remaining original and complete set of 104 issues of* The Jarvey *is kept by the National Library of Ireland in Dublin. They are too fragile for public examination or research but with the financial support of the Heritage Lottery Fund (UK), the Percy French Society has succeeded in having the 104 issues reproduced from digital image files supplied by the Library. Using modern computer photographic technologies they are reproduced in hard-backed volumes and are available for research both at the National Library of Ireland in Dublin, and the Linenhall Library in Belfast.*

Many other publications, references and images used in this study are taken from the Percy French Collection which is cared for by the North Down Museum, Bangor, Co. Down on behalf of the Percy French Society. The Collection comprises some one hundred watercolours together with upwards of eight hundred items of memorabilia relating to the life of Percy French and can be viewed for research by prior arrangement with the Museum.

12. THE OLD CURIOSITY SHOP

Finding another source of income would have been vitally important for the recently married couple, especially as French put it later in life, 'the greatest event in a woman's life was only a few months ahead'. It must have been around this anxious period, probably between his departure from the editorship of *The Jarvey* and the meeting with Dr Houston Collisson, when a charming if rather pathetic interlude in the short marriage of Willie and Ettie French emerged, one which was to lead to a major musical success towards the end of April in the fateful year of 1891. In a paper to the Old Dublin Society many years later, a certain J.W. Hammond recounted how as a boy he once became acquainted with the Percy French who had opened the Old Curiosity Shop at 31 Little Denmark Street in Dublin.

> I can still recollect seeing him in his new Trilby hat, dark coat and grey trousers, standing leisurely within the doorway, hands behind his back, while chatting with a charming vision in a dainty coloured frock – slim, divinely fair, but with that faintly pink complexion indicative of an early call to the Eternal Land of the Ever Young.
>
> The energetic Percy and his delicate young wife only became on speaking terms with me when they had noticed that I used to stand outside their shop every fine day after school hours, watching him sketching at his easel just inside the open door. The predominant feature of Percy's 'Old Curiosity Shop' was pictures – engravings, sketches, paintings in oils and in watercolours … Although then interested in pictures of sailing ships – probably because one of my ancestors had been a shipbuilder with Cardiff and Kehoe on Rogerson's Quay in the 1790s – my own secret attraction in the 'The Old Curiosity Shop' was nothing more than the feathered head-gear of a Red Indian chieftain, which was on a ledge behind Percy's easel. I thought myself a great fellow to have seen real Redskin's plumes, because my parents would not allow me to read the 'Buffalo Bills' and such-like 'Penny Horribles' which delighted boys like me in the 'Gay Nineties'.

Occasionally Mrs French used to send me to McCourt's confectionery shop, next door to Arnott's in Henry Street, for either sixpence or a shilling's worth of the then new Cadbury's Cream Chocolate. Whenever that happened she either shared it with me or gave me a penny or two for myself … One day when Percy was alone in his shop he beckoned me in and asked me what sort of pictures I liked best. As he appeared to me then to be about the same age as my father, I was afraid to tell him 'Cowboys and Redskins', so I said 'Sailing Ships'. He then showed me the only sketch of one that he had and asked me what sort of ship it was. When I told him it was a brig, he looked down on me and smiled. 'It's easy to know that your home must be near Annie Liffey's', he said. Wondering who Annie Liffey was, I shook my head and told him we lived in Stafford Street ... After about two weeks' neglect to pay my customary visit, I went around again one afternoon for to have another study of the Redskin's plumes and to count the number of feathers in it, which I had never done before. But when I arrived there my boyish heart sank! 'The Old Curiosity Shop' was closed up. Everything was gone, except its name above the empty windows. I would never see the Redskin's plumes again; and so the glory of the place to my boyish mentality was extinguished for ever.

'The Artist's Brush'
Watercolour by Percy French
Percy French Collection North Down Museum

Interestingly, Percy French never mentioned the Old Curiosity Shop in his writings. It was most likely a brief and in retrospect unimportant episode in the context of the events that would follow. But before departing from the story it is worth reflecting that the Red Indian headdress, which was the 'secret attraction' for young Hammond, had once been in Cloonyquin. It was brought there by Percy French's great-great-grandfather, Lt. Col. Christopher French who, as already mentioned, was involved in the American Revolution. Also to be noted is the way a relationship grew between French and the boy who returned time after time to enjoy his 'secret attraction', the encounter that would be remembered so vividly some sixty years later.

'Daffodils'
Watercolour by Percy French
Percy French Collection North Down Museum

Paradise

Somewhere east of the Euphrates,
Hidden now from human eyes,
Men tell me that the gate is
Of an earthly Paradise.

Some scorn the ancient story –
Vague tales of long ago,
But I have seen the glory –
I have been there – and I know.

I have found it – I have found it,
Though now 'tis but a dream,
I know the woods that bound it,
I know the silver stream.

Sweet thoughts we two were thinking
As we wandered hand in hand,
And, as the sun was sinking,
We found Enchanted Land.

She turned to me and kissed me,
With love light in her eyes,
Oh, wealth and fame have missed me,
But I've been in Paradise!

Not east of the Euphrates,
Nor guarded from above,
Ah, no, the Golden Gate is
Where Love has answered Love.

And high born hearts and lowly,
May find these fields and know,
The song serene and holy,
Our hearts heard long ago.

The shades of night were falling,
E'en then across her way,
She heard the Angels calling,
She wept – but might not stay.

So when the shadows hide me,
And darkness veils mine eyes,
Sweet Spirit, come and guide me,
Once more to Paradise.

13. TRIUMPH AND TRAGEDY

Anyway, in almost bewildering fashion, from the shadows emerged that larger than life figure, Dr W. Houston Collisson Mus.Doc., who apparently out of the blue, asked or suggested that French write the libretto for a musical comedy in an Irish setting.

William Houston Collisson B.A. Mus.Doc. (Dublin), L. Mus. Trin. Coll. London was born on 20 May 1865 and had just achieved his Mus.Doc. at the age of only twenty-five. He was a successful organist and choir director at a number of large churches where people flocked to enjoy his skills as a musician. He inaugurated the Dublin Popular Concerts at the Antient Concert Rooms and at the Rotunda. These concerts were subsequently extended to Belfast, Londonderry and Cork. Even more impressively, he was conductor and manager of the London Saturday Evening Concerts, which had high quality vocalists and instrumentalists and did tours of towns in Ireland, England and Scotland.

Dr W.H. Collisson
Percy French
Collection North
Down Museum

Essentially a showman, Collisson would play a major role in the life of Percy French in 1891 and also in the years to come. Later in his autobiographical book *Dr Collisson In and On Ireland* the author remembered glowingly how: 'in 1891 a well known name became inseparably linked with mine, the name of Percy French – author, poet, humorist, painter, engineer, mathematician, entertainer and best of men. No living man has got such a grasp on real Irish humour … his humour is never forced, but always subtle.' French himself would surely have baulked at the 'mathematician' label!

With his bottomless mixture of talents and optimism, French took on this new challenge of a comic opera, basing his libretto for *The Knight of the Road* on the career of a legendary Irish highwayman, Jack Freeney. Thanks to Dr Collisson's influence with musical societies, an orchestra and chorus were quickly assembled. The only paid professionals in the cast were Henry Beaumont and Miss Dubedat. French himself played the leading role, helped no doubt by his insider's knowledge as librettist combined with a well-established ability to extemporise. Two weeks at the Queen's Theatre and the support of the Dublin papers led to packed houses each night with even the 'vice-royalty' attending for one performance.

Far left:

French as Jack Freeney in The Knight of the Road

Percy French Collection North Down Museum

The Knight of the Road poster

Percy French Collection North Down Museum

Also, at that time, the *Handbook of the Irish Parliament Houses* as published by one H. Goldsmith Whitton. It contained contributions by W.P. French and was illustrated by his friend, R.C. Orpen and by Mrs Ethel French, French's newly-wed wife. The architecturally splendid Parliament Buildings, no longer needed for their original purpose after the Act of Union in 1801, had by then become the headquarters of the Bank of Ireland.

These lines from French's parody of Edgar Allen Poe's 'A Long Way' suggests that had French been around he might not have been quite in favour of the Act, for which he mainly allocated the blame to the then Prime Minister, William Pitt:

> *But evil days, rebellious factions,*
> *Rose on fair Hibernia's Isle,*
> *Bribery controlled their actions,*
> *Honesty gave way to guile;*
> *All the grandeur and the glory*
> *Where the members used to sit*
> *Were – you all may read the story,*
> *Swallowed by the Pitt.*

The *Handbook of the Irish Parliament Houses* contained an impressive illustration of the still-intact House of Lords by R.C. Orpen and an equally finely drawn depiction of the entrance and courtyard of the splendid building signed 'E.K.F.' (Mrs Ethel French).

Entrance and courtyard of the former Irish Parliament Houses now Bank of Ireland, College Green, Dublin

Drawing by Mrs E.K. French from The Handbook of the Irish Parliament Houses *by H. Goldsmith Whitton*

With the birth of a baby to the young wife now imminent, Willie and Ettie returned to the home of Colonel and Mrs Howard Brooke in the Vale of Avoca in Co. Wicklow, the location of their not too distant honeymoon. From this scenic setting Ettie sent sketches of 'that most lovely spot' to her sister-in-law to be, Mrs De Burgh Daly. Ethel (Ettie) may have caught a chill either there or on their return journey; at that time part of the travel at least would have been by sidecar. Their daughter was born on 5 June 1891. Both Ettie and their daughter tragically died, Ettie of septicaemia on 29 June, a year and a day after their wedding, and the baby girl on 5 July at Cloonyquin.

One can only make a feeble guess at the depth of despair and grief experienced by French as he gazed dumbstruck at the body of his young wife and 'ray of sunshine' lying with 'lips cold and white'. French, as his sister Mrs De Burgh Daly has written, was a very reserved man who expressed his feelings more easily in verse such as the poem, 'Only Goodnight':

> *Only 'goodnight' sweet heart,*
> *And not farewell,*
> *Though for all times thou art*
> *Where Angels dwell.*
>
> *Though for a time those eyes*
> *Lose their soft light,*
> *Let there be no good-byes,*
> *Only goodnight.*
>
> *Though for a time they toll*
> *Thy passing bell,*
> *'Tis but goodnight, sweet soul,*
> *And not farewell.*
>
> *O'er thy sweet lips I sigh –*
> *Lips cold and white,*
> *There! – that is not good-bye.*
> *Only 'goodnight'.*

A headstone at Dublin's Mount Jerome Cemetery has engraved thereon:

'Ethel, the beloved wife of W. Percy French, who died June 29th 1891' followed by:

Rest – sleep came early, better so,
Since waking means but weeping;
And we who still the struggle know,
Half envy thee thy sleeping.

Rest – never to the silent sod,
A kindlier heart was given;
No purer soul returns to God
No sweeter life to Heaven.

A visit organized by Alan Tongue for the Percy French Society to that special place in Mount Jerome cemetery in Dublin in 1992 was a moving experience as indeed was a later visit to the lovely little hilltop church at Conary above Castle Howard where French and Ettie would have enjoyed the scenic views. A lectern had been installed in the Church: 'In memoriam E.K. French. She left us 29th June 1891.'

French, by all accounts, disappeared from the public eye thereafter. According to his daughter Ettie he 'took his bicycle' and went to North Wales but there is no record at all of what he did or where precisely he was at this traumatic time. Subsequently his hair would change from brown to white.

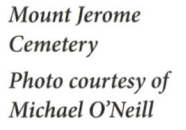

Mount Jerome Cemetery

Photo courtesy of Michael O'Neill

But, as daughter Ettie put it, 'he was never an escapist and August 1891 saw him back in Dublin for a revival of *The Knight of the Road* in Horse Show week.' It is also known that he lived at The Mall, Strand Road, Baldoyle, Co. Dublin from time to time afterwards. There he painted local seascapes, many of them on the door panels of Mrs Hanley's house. At Baldoyle he was 'out catching impressions of sky, wave and shore' leading to his second most popular painting theme 'The Breaking Wave'. Later, in a letter from this setting to Helen (Lennie) Sheldon, his wife to be, he mentions in passing, 'This is a wonderful place for skies – a cargo of ten masterpieces sent to Belfast.'

'The Breaking Wave'

Watercolour by Percy French

Percy French Collection North Down Museum

14. LIFE GOES ON, AS IT MUST

The tragic loss of his young wife can only have been a huge watershed in the emotional life of Percy French. The rather happy-go-lucky 'gifted amateur' approach would over a period give way to a slightly more professional attitude to life and to a career in the entertainment world. Clearly the success of *The Knight of the Road*, or *The Irish Girl* as it was subsequently designated, was an encouragement to continue along the road of comic opera, becoming perhaps an Irish equivalent of Gilbert and Sullivan across the Irish Sea. Musically, French believed it was the best that 'the doctor' (i.e. Collisson) had ever done and, even though not usually given to blowing his own trumpet, French felt his libretto 'measured up to most'.

On the crest of this wave, French and Collisson quickly composed the musical comedy *Strongbow*. The story was based on the episode in the history of Ireland as was mentioned at the outset of this story of the life and times of Percy French. The show drew good crowds in its first week. In an upbeat interview with the *Evening Telegraph* French, who played the part of a harper, spoke of how the producer, Mr Whitbread, hoped to see it staged at one of the London theatres. But already the critics in the Dublin papers were taking the line that the subject of the opera was not 'happily chosen' and that such a serious event in Irish history should not be treated so lightly. Amongst other things French had inferred that the real life Strongbow and his cohorts had come to Ireland by invitation. Although partially true, this angle was apparently not the accepted interpretation at the time. Sadly this interlude brought the French/Collisson musical comedy bandwagon to a full stop in Dublin, although they had not given up hope of a London impresario taking *Strongbow* on board.

The collaboration did continue though in less ambitious ways, for instance, as a flyer for a show at Dublin's Leinster Hall indicated. A piece in the *Tyrone Constitution* of the time also gave a positive account of an entertainment at the Grand Jury Rooms at Omagh. Amongst the items performed were French singing his new compositions 'Soldiers Three' and 'The Night That Miss Cooney Eloped' (the latter with each character in caricature appearing on the lantern screen).

Song cover: Soldiers Three

Percy French Collection North Down Museum

The 'Cooney' song was based on a growing class-consciousness. In this case a Miss Cooney upsets her family by eloping with the chimney sweep. Most accounts of French's life contain a story about a real Cooney family who had undergone exactly such an event and were in fact in the audience on the occasion of French's singing of his song. Not too surprisingly, they were left in proverbial high dudgeon. It seems rather too much of a coincidence, but why spoil such a much-loved anecdote!

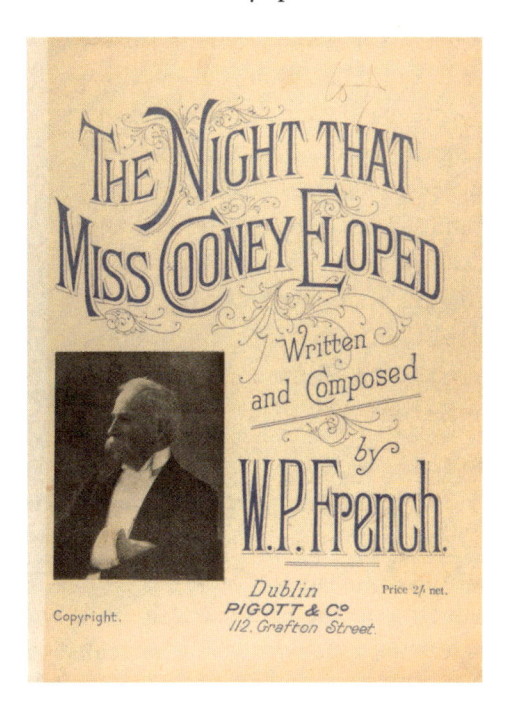

Song cover 'The Night that Miss Cooney Eloped'

Percy French Collection North Down Museum

French also amused the audience with his tale about his failure as an engineer and, with his own banjo accompaniment, sang the songs of the 'Mississippi Shore'. Dr Collisson's piano playing, which included one of Mendelssohn's compositions, got much applause, though French by way of jest announced he would not be responsible for it. This was an excellent programme of entertainment ending with some sidelights on Irish life, further comic illustrations shown by the 'powerful oxy-hydrogen lantern' operated by that ever-supportive friend and partner, Richard C. (Dick) Orpen.

*Harry Furniss
1854-1925*

Advertisement for 'Irish Lights and Shadows' Courthouse, Ballyconnell, 25 February 1897

Percy French Society Archive

It was during a visit to a lantern lecture given by Harry Furniss (a famous Punch artist) on the London Parliament that Orpen suggested French write a lecture on Dublin which he, Orpen, would illustrate with caricatures of celebrities (they had them in those days too!). In no time they had appeared in the Antient Concert Rooms with a lantern lecture called 'Dublin Up-to-Date'. In French's own words:

> I began 'ladies and gentlemen, there are two sides to everything – except Harcourt Street Station.' What a small joke – but Heavens! what a laugh! It taught me the value of topical allusions. Orpen's pictures got round after round of applause, and during the interval he and his young brother 'Billy' drew lightning sketches in coloured chalks. 'Dublin Up-to-Date' went on tour and as Dick Orpen, being a rising young architect, could not come, I devised a comic landscape in coloured chalks which I gave as an interlude. And then the decisive and fateful reasoning: that mighty ovation told me that if there was no demand for me as an engineer, I might yet succeed as an entertainer.

The basic elements of French's future recitals – various titles such as 'Song, Story and Sketch', 'Social Absurdities' and other 'W. Percy French Entertainments' – had emerged. Soon performances in towns such as Athlone and Kilkenny received unstinted praise from the press, who drew favourable comparisons with such famous one-man entertainers as Du Val and George Grossmith. This was the time when French decided to earn a living as a professional entertainer.

15. HELEN (LENNIE) SHELDON

However, something else was also underway in the life and times of Percy French. Although the comic opera Strongbow had ended in a negative matter, a positive outcome would emerge through the presence of a young English lady in the chorus. She was a friend of Alice Linde, one of the principal singers. Her name was Helen Sheldon of Burmington House, Warwickshire, and there followed a romantic courtship of Helen (Lennie) by French. The courtship was conducted by occasional visits to Warwickshire but mainly by letters, writings that tell us much about the innermost character of French, revealing the deepest of feelings as well as insights that are reserved for only the closest relationships. A sense of the forlorn and the need for female companionship is typically balanced with humorous comment; soon he would arrive at 'the fleshpots of Burmington'. One thing is quite clear, he did not try to hide his state of impecuniousness: he 'hadn't the price of a cup of tea' or was 'trying to avoid ticket collectors!' It put a huge focus on whatever other qualities he may have had as a potential life companion. His emerging forgetfulness was also becoming evident: 'My other shoe left London on Tuesday for Burmington so I am still on the hop.'

Alice Linde
Percy French Collection North Down Museum

'Lennie'
Drawing by Walter Osborne R.H.A. 1859-1903
Percy French Collection North Down Museum

During the courtship (1892-3) and before his decision to become a professional entertainer, French spent much time in London. He was trying with Collisson to interest people such as D'Oyly Carte in the *Strongbow* musical comedy, but without success. They did give a concert there and attended some theatres. French's love letters to Lennie became more intimate and relaxed and are signed 'Willie.' One to 'Darling Lennie' mentioned his old and learned friend, A.D. Godley: 'I see Godley's poem reviewed in the *Pall Mall* – they call them clever but only to be understood by Oxfordmen'. This is another indication of French the entertainer's lack of interest in the classical or the elite.

As well as his love for Lennie, these letters reveal how frugally he was getting by in London while 'trying my best to collect feathers for our little nest'. He was sketching by day and writing by night. However, he did go to *In Town*, where he saw Loie Fuller. He writes, 'She is very nice but I don't think my mother would approve of her'. Lennie's 'wandering sweetheart, Willie' also spent some time at Lynmouth in Devon where there was a well established school of painters, a school also frequented by Richard Orpen. He had his bicycle with him to help with travel costs and he wrote, 'I only wish my talents lay in a more money making groove.' There were occasional visits to Warwickshire to see Lennie and to undertake the delicate business of convincing her parents.

'River and Boat'
Watercolour by Percy French
Percy French Collection North Down Museum

Far left: 'Moonlit Coast'

Watercolour by Percy French

Percy French Collection North Down Museum

'Newlyn by Night'

Watercolour by R.C. Orpen R.H.A. 1863-1938

Percy French Collection North Down Museum

According to her eldest daughter, Lennie was musical and an unusually good pianist, interested in writing and sketching and with a strong sense of family. It is likely that at this time Percy French saw himself mostly as a writer, a vocation that might have been more acceptable to Lennie's family. However, one senses that he was not convinced that he should make the necessary effort to 'join the club'. After attending the annual dinner of the Society of Authors, he wrote to Lennie: 'I wore my black, cut rather low and filled in with 3ply linen. I also wore a false smile to ingratiate myself with the company and help conceal my ears; a harlequin set of studs and hair parted on the bias completed my costume.' This 'dressing up' must surely have been a major effort by one not known for any kind of sartorial interest, one capable of travelling from Dublin to London in his slippers!

On 24 January 1894 W. Percy French, then aged thirty-nine, and Helen (Lennie) Sheldon, aged twenty-five, were married in Burmington. The wedding had rather more traditional trappings than the occasion of his first marriage to Ethel (Ettie) Armytage Moore. The bridegroom called on one of his earliest friends to be best man: A.D. Godley, who for the occasion carried the contrasting distinctions of Dean of Magdalen College, Oxford and contributor to the home-produced MS magazine The Trombone of Truth.

'Mollie'
Watercolour by Percy French
Percy French Collection North Down Museum

Their first home was a studio apartment in Dublin's Dawson Street. Later Willie and Lennie moved to 35 Mespil Road. 'We are living by the canal – do drop in', he wrote to his friends. On 4 November 1894 a daughter was born and named Ethel Gwendoline thereby keeping in mind for perpetuity the memory of Ethel (Ettie) Armytage Moore. A telegram to a friend read, 'A small French lady came last night – find it hard to make her understand our language – all well'. The new arrival would always be called 'Ettie' and it is to her we are happily beholden for her memoir *Willie*, a tribute to her father written with clarity and perception when she was in her mid-nineties. A second daughter Mollie was born on 13 March 1896 and a third daughter Joan would arrive some years later on 26 April 1903, after the family had moved to London.

'By the Canal'
Watercolour by Percy French
Courtesy of Co. Roscommon Percy French Society

16. THE PROFESSIONAL ENTERTAINER

For the now-happily married man the 1890s continued creatively and prolifically. The emphasis was on his income-producing work as an entertainer. He was honoured with a 'benefit concert' in 1895 in which he himself took part together with friends from the world of entertainment, such as Orpen, Collisson, Hamilton and Alice Linde. The song 'Drumcolliher', a song whose contrast between the grandeur of London life and the simpler values of a small town in Ireland we still enjoy so much today, was a sign that French's world was extending to England. The new song 'Mulligan's Masquerade' was a tilt at the more pompous masked balls of the era, whilst the lesser known 'Killyran Wrackers' together with songs by John Count McCormack serve as a behind the lines World War II battle hymn for the legendary Lt. Col. 'Paddy' Blair Mayne, DSO, of Newtownards, Co. Down, a founder of the Special Air Service and a former Irish international rugby football player.

> *But from the field of glory will come another story,*
> *And Colonel Kit Magorey gives me to understan'*
> *No foe will ever face us, if only in the van*
> *Is that mob of malefactors from the town of Killyran,*
> *And if the Kaiser ever tries the flame of war to fan,*
> *Berlin will be bombarded by the Boys of Killyran.*

During this prolific decade, French the watercolour artist had some twenty-four paintings exhibited at the Royal Hibernian Academy. The more expensive ones included 'Lough Cara', 'Roscommon' and 'Portumna, Lough Derg'. As an indication of the difficulty of evaluating French the artist independently from his work as writer and poet, one exhibit was entitled in verse:

> *Only the sullen seas that flow*
> *And ebb for evermore*
> *But tarry awhile sad heart and lo!*
> *A light on that lonely shore.*

In these lines can also be discerned a sense of sadness and melancholy, an underlying trait that had been more acutely exposed by French's harrowing experience just a few years earlier. Meanwhile in 1897 Dr Collisson had taken Holy Orders in the Church of England and moved to parish work in Cornwall. But that would not be the end of either the musical collaboration or the valued friendship between him and French; Collisson later moved to a London parish.

In his book *Dr Collisson In and On Ireland*, under the heading 'Together with Percy French in London early 1900s', Dr Collisson contributes the following anecdote:

> I once got Percy French an engagement for a political meeting. The hall was so crowded that he could not even get inside the door and there was no entrance from the platform end of the hall. As I was responsible for the programme I was in despair when I could not find him. Presently we saw a leg coming through a window over the platform, then a ladder was thrust through, and our humorist descended the ladder amidst a bevy of Members of Parliament and their wives. It was an ideal entrance for a comic man, and he never performed more brilliantly than he did on that occasion.

French the professional entertainer

Percy French Collection North Down Museum

The 1890s also saw the publishing of the enduring songs 'Eileen Oge – The Pride of Petravore' (music arranged by Collisson) and 'McBreen's Heifer'. As with most of French's songs they contain a homely moral or a lesson to be learned: mainly, do not prolong your courting! Jamesy O'Byrne spends too long weighing the very contrasting merits of McBreen's daughters whilst for Eileen Oge it is the 'hard faced' but 'big and masterful' cattle jobber that wins the day after others are overcome by shyness in the face of her beauty. In 1900, encouraged by Collisson, French wrote 'When Erin Awakes' – his only foray into the romantic vision of ancient Ireland. Set to music by Collisson, the song won the award for the best arrangement of an Irish melody in that year's Dublin Feis Ceoil.

French formally dressed
Percy French Collection North Down Museum

Meanwhile his entertainments, ever eclectic, often included 'Mr Martin', an expert on the copophone (musical glasses). French's ingenuity at developing and writing new material was endless and the song 'Mat Hanigan's Aunt' emerged at this time. It received a good press: 'one of the best of his songs is "Mat Hanigan's Aunt" which the author renders in fetching fashion, accompanying himself on the banjo.' It started robustly:

> Here's a health to Hanigan's Aunt,
> And I'll tell you the reason why,
> She always kept things decent in the Hanigan familie,
> A platter and can for every man
> What more could the quality want?
> Ye've your bit and your sup,
> What's cockin' ye up,
> Says Matthew Hanigan's Aunt.

Song cover 'Mat Hanigan's Aunt'
Percy French Collection North Down Museum

One might wonder what his inspiration was for 'Mat Hanigan's Aunt'. Serendipitously, *The Irish Book Lover* (Vol. 29) of May 1943 mentions some verses published in 1839 (before French was born) in a book by Charles Lever:

> Here's health to Martin Hanegan's Aunt,
> And I'll tell you the reason why!
> She eats bekase she is hungry
> And drinks bekase she is dry,
> And if ever a man,
> Stopped the course of a can,
> Martin Hanegan's Aunt would cry –
> 'Arragh, fill up your glass,
> And let the jug pass;
> How d'ye know but your neighbour's dhry?'

Home Rule cartoon from The Jarvey
Percy French Collection North Down Museum

And so an old drinking song was rewritten and published by W.P. French, barely disguised and rearranged to suit his banjo and to emphasize the consumption of food rather than ale (again an indication of his dislike of alcohol!). Somewhat similarly, his 'New Comic Song – Ben Bolt' caused a degree of laughter when it was mentioned at the British Library (Music Section); their old song books showed that 'Ben Bolt' was written in 1848, before French was born! He was nothing if not adaptive and innovative.

Meanwhile politics at Westminster and the matter of Home Rule for Ireland were presumably of little import as French worked night and day to establish a career and make a living for his family. Nonetheless, there are indications of French's all-round awareness. For example, he spontaneously composed a limerick based on the word 'Kilcoole', suggested by a member of an audience:

> There was an old man of Kilcoole
> Who married a wife, quite a fool.
> 'Twas a union,' he'd say,
> 'That I wanted that day,
> But begorrah I'm getting Home Rule.'

Successful performances in Ireland in locations of varying degrees of sophistication – from the Lord Lieutenant's residence at the Vice-Regal Lodge to the more homely ambience of the village of Dunlavin in Co.Wicklow – eventually led to occasional engagements in England. We learn from Jim McDowell's book *Beyond the Lights* that Percy French was highly regarded by London's 'Father of Music Hall' Charles Morton. 'Percy French – the Irish Entertainer' was performing regularly in Morton's Palace of Varieties towards the end of the 1890s. In 1899 a series of French's 'Recitals' in London were greeted positively by the press and he was persuaded by his agent, Gerald Christie, to make a career move to the metropolis. Already he had been performing there at the city's famous meeting place of entertainers, the Savage Club. A new way of life was on the horizon for Percy French and family and in January 1900 they moved to live at 21 Clifton Hill, St John's Wood, London.

Theatre of Varieties programmes

Percy French Collection North Down Museum

17. THE WEST CLARE RAILWAY

Ye may talk of Columbus's sailing
Across the Atlantical sea
But he never tried to go railing
From Ennis as far as Kilkee.

'The divil a thrain!'
Cartoon by Percy French
Percy French Collection North Down Museum

In 1896 or thereabouts Percy French, now a professional entertainer, left Broadstone terminus in Dublin on the Midland Great Western Railway to fulfil an engagement in far-away Kilkee on the west coast of Ireland. At Ennis, Co. Clare, he joined the narrow gauge West Clare Railway in order to complete the journey to Kilkee. The smaller train developed engine trouble at Miltown Malbay (having taken weeds as well as water into the boiler). Despite phone calls and efforts by staff, a replacement engine failed to materialise. French was late for his advertised performance; his 'magic lantern' was further delayed and many of those assembled for the show had departed by the time he got underway at Moore's Concert Hall.

French must have had strong feelings about his loss of earnings and damage to his growing professional reputation because he sued the West Clare Railway Company, an action that would have required costly legal representation and as well as travel to the court case held on the following year. At the court proceedings – reported in the Clare Journal – the judge was apparently more favourably disposed towards the plaintiff than towards the Railway Company. Asked by defence counsel whether the Hall would have been full 'His Honour' intervened to express the view that it would have been, if the audience had not been drinking whiskey in the local pubs for which, he interjected, there were too many licences being issued. Amusingly, he continued, Kilkee was a 'watering place' where very little water was consumed. Here was this gentleman coming down from Dublin, he went on, to improve life there by creating a taste for 'national entertainment' and the Railway Company had resisted the gentleman's claim. The judge awarded £10 damages plus expenses.

The Railway Company subsequently lost an appeal against the judgement. At the appeal it was discovered that not only did French's current entertainment programme, *Society Sketches*, have a section on 'Our Railways', but he had also written a song about his experiences on the West Clare Railway:

> *If you want to get to Kilkee*
> *You must go there by sea,*
> *And not by the Wild West Clare.*

Laughter followed in court, before the judge, tongue-in-cheek, suggested that French take care not to represent the trial and court case in his next entertainment!

The song mentioned in the court case was not the famous song 'Are Ye Right There, Michael?', which is so much associated with the songwriter today. It was written some five years later, by which time French was living in London. The music for 'Are Ye Right There, Michael?' was initially composed by Dr Houston Collisson and then more successfully rewritten by French himself. The overall outcome beautifully conveys the staccato movement of the train combined with that sleepy sound of voices communicating in the local idiom in the background. Although a send-up of certain inefficiencies, there is gentleness in the humour that makes Michael and company lovable as they struggle with the problems of keeping the service going.

We even enjoy the route through 'Sweet Corofin' and 'Lahinch' where 'the sea shines like a jewel' and of course, 'Kilkee', which from French's first hand experience, 'Oh, you never get near it.' Overall the song is a mine of social history not just about West Clare but of much of the Ireland of the time. It's about a relatively new railway system, the difficulties of coping with railway time as opposed to local time and a network that would be ever more important to the career of Percy French and to Irish life in general. It's also about a time with more emphasis on human values, as indicated by the concern shown by Michael for the parcel expected for 'Mrs White.' According to Thomas Mason, who often travelled with French in those days, on another occasion the train was held up at a wayside station. It was a very hot day and the stationmaster pumped glasses of water from a nearby well to quench the passengers' thirst. Most importantly, the song reminds us again of French's way of channelling irritation or frustration into philosophical humour with a memorable outcome.

Note: *The West Clare Railway, which closed in 1961, has partially reopened in recent years as a tourist attaction. An original engine, the Slieve Callan, has been beautifully restored and was returned to Moyasta Junction in 2009.*

18. 'THIS LONDON'S A WONDERFUL SIGHT'

Percy French's daughter Ettie, herself an entertainer of real talent and stage presence, has written with authority on the English world of entertainment at the beginning of the twentieth century. Two major currents of activity were emerging. There was the world of private entertaining, which rose to its highest pitch during this Edwardian period. No home or garden party was complete without a performance of some sort. Meanwhile, the growth of lecture societies was a further opportunity to provide occasional evenings of fun combined with art. Her father's show was 'a gift' to both forms of entertainment:

> Willie's versatility was, and perhaps remains unique. This entertainer who sang Irish songs to the banjo, then showed his talent as a comic draughtsman, came back again to impersonate a terrified guest at a children's party, and wound up by painting a romantic landscape upside down, was something quite new.

'Westminster from the Thames'
Watercolour by Percy French
Percy French Collection North Down Museum

There were other engagements as well: public school and college entertainments, dinners and regular recitals at the Steinway Hall. Despite such an avalanche of new opportunities, Percy French impressively demonstrated his love of the less glamorous side of life by returning to Ireland every summer for a month or more to tour the coastal resorts ('watering places'). Perhaps it was his ability to relate to people as individuals that enabled him to be comfortable and accepted in such contrasting locations. This contrast is indelibly commemorated in one of his most successful songs 'The Mountains o' Mourne', composed in 1902 at 21 Clifton Hill. In his own words:

French in formal pose
Percy French Collection North Down Museum

> Looking at the range of the Mourne Mountains from Skerries one clear afternoon I found myself repeating, 'the Mountains of Mourne sweep down to the sea.' This line kept recurring to me till one day it wedded itself to an old Irish air, and the combination seemed so happy that I set to work, or rather shut myself in my top room with pen, ink and paper, and waited. Presently the idea entered my head that such a refrain might be sung by an exile from Erin – Lord Northcliffe's dictum that you interest the greatest number of people if you talk about love, or about London, also occurred to me at the time; and so my most successful song, admirably arranged by Dr Collisson, was given to an applauding public.

> *Oh, Mary this London's a wonderful sight,*
> *Wid the people here workin' by day and by night;*
> *They don't sow potatoes, nor barley, nor wheat,*
> *But there's gangs o' them diggin' for gold in the street;*
> *At least, when I axed them that's what I was told,*
> *So I just took a hand at this diggin' for gold,*
> *But for all that I found there I might as well be,*
> *Where the Mountains o' Mourne sweep down to the sea.*

The song continues with four more verses in which the clash of cultures is further explored with a perceptive humour. Despite the obvious commercial intention for his song, a somewhat discordant note is struck in the third verse. As is often the case with French, it is as if he feels it necessary to insert a note of reality to leaven any sense of comfortable sentimentality:

I seen England's King from the top of a 'bus –
I never knew him, though he means to know us;
And though by the Saxon we once were oppressed,
Still I cheered – God forgive me! – I cheered wid the rest.
And now that he's visited Erin's green shore,
We'll be much better friends than we've been heretofore,
When we've got all we want we're as quiet as can be
Where the Mountains o' Mourne sweep down to the sea.

This verse contains an innocent expression of somewhat contradictory feelings by the 'exile'. Although at the time the King's dominion was over a United Kingdom of Great Britain and Ireland, the 'exile' refers to him as 'England's King' whilst at the same time inferring that 'oppression' was in the past. There is an inclination to cheer, notwithstanding any such reservations, and a colonial attitude is evident in the line 'When we've got all we want we're as quiet as can be'. One might easily empathise with Pigotts, the publisher, who initially turned the song down because it was 'not serious enough for a ballad, not funny enough for a comic song'. Not too surprisingly, the many interpreters of French's work rarely, if ever, use the third verse. As ever in successful song writing, it is that word picture of the 'Mountains o' Mourne' combined with a lovely traditional air, rearranged as it was by Houston Collisson, that provides us with one of French's best loved songs.

'The Mournes from Royal County Down Golf Club'

Watercolour by Percy French

Percy French Collection North Down Museum

Interestingly, the reference to the King confirms that the song was composed after the death of Queen Victoria in 1901 and after King Edward VII had ascended the throne. It was also subsequent to the King's visit to 'Ireland's green shore' after his coronation in 1902. Thus the inaccurate but commonly held view that the song was written in 1896 can be finally refuted (the original song sheet has in any case an address of 21 Clifton Hill, where French and family lived after their move to London in 1900).

His daughter tells us that 'the cachet of a Royal Command was bestowed on him within two years of his arrival, so his success was assured', notwithstanding such references in his famous song. 1902 was coronation year and entertaining embarked on a period of prosperity. Percy French, 'the Irish Entertainer', was on his way despite, according to his daughter, never having had a lesson in singing, drawing or painting. An hour's coaching with a banjo expert now and then was his sole effort in improving his stage technique. In spite of his elevation to such heights of cosmopolitan success, he did not forsake his old stamping ground at Dublin's Antient Concert Rooms. In January 1902 'Mr. Percy French's Recital, as given before His Majesty the King, and T.R.H. the Prince and Princess of Wales' took place. Always humorous and never one to eschew the importance of advertising and publicity, he had an artistically designed flyer that confidently announced 'The Next Landing of the French'. This was his parody of an old Irish rebel ballad that once had forecast an invasion by the French army:

> *Oh! the French is on the say, Says the Shan Van Voght*
> *He'll be here without delay, says the Shan Van Voght*
> *He's been gone for many a day,*
> *By them Saxons led astray,*
> *Och! sure them's the boys can pay! Says the Shan Van Voght.*
>
> *(Shan Van Voght – anglicized = Sean-bhean Bhocht = Poor Old Woman = Ireland)*

19. TOWARDS THE PEAK OF HIS CAREER

There can be little doubt that Percy French's wife, Lennie, brought elements of order, support and stability to the life of her husband. She combined qualities of good humour, an awareness of current affairs and a sense of family with an interest in writing, sketching and music and she was, according to her daughter, 'an unusually good pianist.' Ironically, her own comfortable family background was sustained by businesses such as wine merchanting and milling; horror of horrors, they were 'in trade'. She would, theoretically at least, have 'looked up' to one of the landed (i.e. 'stranded') gentry! There was perhaps one ironic, if tenuous, redeeming feature: it is believed that an ancestor of Lennie's was Lord Mayor of Dublin in 1691, the same year that Arthur French, the important ancestor of Percy French, was mayor of Galway.

From the outset of their London life, Lennie kept a diary of French's engagements side by side with notes on their social and family activities. With the assistance of an agent, her husband's entertainment career developed with breath-taking speed and was not at all confined to London. Apart from private parties and other engagements around London, such place names as Howth, Portarlington, Bradford, Harwich and Brighton Pavilion appear as early as the months July to December 1900. Lennie's closely written lines in the diaries show her husband ever busier in 1901 and 1902. Leeds, Shrewsbury, Nottingham, and Formby in England; Dumfries and Motherwell in Scotland; and such Percy French-associated Irish stamping grounds as Kilkee, Rosses Point, Youghal and Portrush were just a few of the locations that he visited. This is not to mention a stop-off at his birthplace at Cloonyquin. Engagements in Pontyprid and Cardiff showed that no part of the United Kingdom, as then constituted, was unaware of his growing reputation. Such immense success involved a huge amount of travelling – from Glasgow to Folkstone and from Wexford to Portrush. Only the widespread Victorian railway system could have enabled such a career to evolve and flourish so quickly.

Towards the Peak of His Career

And so the scene was set for hugely busy and successful years as a popular entertainer, years that at last brought a worthwhile income, by his standards. Occasionally the diaries show that the intensity of performance and engagement was alleviated by a more exotic event such as dinner at the Savage Club with Lord Roberts or a break away from the city for painting. Brittany became the destination for family holidays.

'Queen Victoria's Entry through Dublin's City Gates'

Watercolour by Percy French

Courtesy of The National Gallery of Ireland

In 1904 French, 'assisted by the well known London entertainer Ernest Denny', gave an impressive 'recital' at Dublin's Antient Concert Rooms. His 'Evening Programme' included his clever parodies of nursery rhymes as they might be written in the style of poets such as Tennyson, Burns, Poe and Kipling as for instance:

Baa Baa Black Sheep (à la Rudyard Kipling) – verse 2:

'Have I wool?' said the Baa Baa Black Sheep,
'You ask me have I wool?
When I yield each year
To the shepherd's shear
As much as three bags full.'

'Guildo, Brittany'
Watercolour by Percy French
Percy French Collection
North Down Museum

Here again French elegantly sends up the established romantic poets in a gentle but pointed way. His matinée performance also included the 'Children's Party', a monologue that was part of French's entertainment programmes for many years. This was, of course, his London based show taken to Dublin, rather than the summer tour entertainments around Ireland that had become such an essential part of his annual calendar.

'A Lion Story' from the 'Children's Party'

Artist unknown

Percy French Society Archive

During the previous August French had visited Connemara (for painting?) and entertained in such coastal centres as Howth, Skerries, Malahide, Warrenpoint, Newcastle, Bangor, Portrush, Ballycastle and Bundoran. It was a time when one could travel from London to Clifden in Connemara on one ticket and one wonders if French's wistful poem 'To the West' relates to the aforementioned visit to Connemara. There is that sense of the lure of Ireland and of the west in particular:

> *The Midland Great Western is doing its best,*
> *And the circular ticket is safe in my vest;*
> *But I feel that my holiday never begins*
> *Till I'm in Connemara among the Twelve Pins.*

And then the final punch lines in which French changes from the formal language to the local idiom as he colourfully contrasts the two very different lifestyles:

> *Tonight when all London's with gaslight agleam,*
> *And the Carlton is filled with Society's cream,*
> *I'll be 'takin' me tay' down at ould Johnny Flinn's,*
> *Safe an' away in the heart o' the Pins.*

'The Twelve Pins'
Watercolour by Percy French
Percy French Collection North Down Museum

20. SONGS, SATIRES AND SPELLS

With Dr Collisson available to arrange the music, a variety of songs such as 'Jim Wheelahan's Automobeel', 'Maguire's Motorbike', 'Donnegan's Daughter', 'Father O'Callaghan' and 'King Edward in Erin' were successfully launched. The first two, 'Jim Wheelahan's Automobeel' and 'Maguire's Motorbike,' concerned the noisy activity and rather bloody downfall of two self-made 'heroes' of the motoring age. 'Donnegan's Daughter' pokes fun at the rather grand ideas of successful emigrants revisiting their hometowns. Donnegan and his 'made-up' daughter adopt a somewhat ostentatious façade upon their return from the States. Inevitably, in Percy French's eye, this cut no ice in Ballyporeen and, on the way home from a dance some 'kissin' and squeezing' caused a fall into a stream that destroyed the daughter's carefully constructed image:

*Song cover
'Jim Wheelahan's Automobeel'
Percy French Collection North Down Museum*

> *For her roses had wilted,*
> *Her wig it was tilted,*
> *The figure she'd built, it*
> *Was washed away clean:*

However, French, in a different mode, also draws attention to the effects of emigration on those who are left behind in 'An Irish Mother' (subsequently put to music by Brendan O'Dowda):

> *A wee slip drawin' water,*
> *Me ould man at the plough.*
> *No grown up son nor daughter,*
> *That's the way we're farmin' now,*
> *'No work and little pleasure'*
> *Was the cry before they wint*
> *Now they're gettin' both full measure,*
> *So I ought to be contint.*
> *Great wages men is givin'*
> *In that land beyant the say.*
> *But 'tis lonely lonely livin'*
> *Whin the childher is away.*

Dr Collisson's mother's maiden name was O'Callaghan, a likely background to 'Father O'Callaghan', a song in praise of the deep humility and kindness of a priest who most likely was known to both French and Collisson. There is nothing comic about this tribute to a saintly personage. The lyrics of 'King Edward in Erin' suggest that the King should receive a positive welcome on the occasion of his 1907 visit:

> *For the King that's come over to see us at last,*
> *Has nothin' to do wid the days that are past*
> *And though there are some that to sorrows will cling,*
> *For a while we'll forget them and welcome the King.*

Song cover
'The Darlin'
Girl from Clare'

Percy French
Collection North
Down Museum

Despite the extra energy and ambition engendered through French's creative partnership with Collisson which resulted in memorable compositions such as 'Mrs Brady' and 'Eileen Oge', other songs such as 'The Oklahoma Rose' (a tuneful 'plantation' style melody) and 'The Darlin' Girl from Clare', composed by French himself, may be deemed of no lesser merit.

'Mrs Brady', however, is a delightful piece of social history about the three suitors of a widow who, as they see it, 'has the land' after 'ould Brady', her husband, has 'gone to glory.' In his most informative lecture on the occasion of the opening of the first Percy French Summer School in 2009, the president of the school Mr Michael D. Higgins (subsequently President of Ireland) spoke of how property ownership had become 'a new reality' after the effects of land consolidation, the famine and emigrant remittances. Mr Higgins also explained that the philosophy of ownership and the resulting competition for land in French's time helped 'create the land war (1879-1882)' and led to 'at least 15 gradations of society.' Percy French looked beneath 'the layers of pretension' that resulted, as is evident in so many of his best-known songs.

Those 'gradations' then emerging in Irish society are reflected in two of French's less well-known but sensitively composed songs 'Phishlin' Phil McHugh' and 'Little Brigid Flynn.' In the former, Mary is waiting patiently for her heart's desire, Phishlin' Phil, who is something of 'a rover'. She is resisting the blandishments of her mother, who favours 'Ten-acre Thady' with his fine newly slated house. Nor is Mary interested in 'Danny Michael Dan who is six fut in his stockin's.' A giant compared to French's own five feet and five inches!

On the other hand, the suitor for 'Little Brigid Flynn' who is 'living all alone' rejects his father's advice 'to get a girl that owns a bit of land'. He already possesses 'a fine slated house and a cow or two at grass.' In these earthly parables by Percy French, it almost goes without saying that despite the social pressures for material betterment a touch of romance can be decisive.

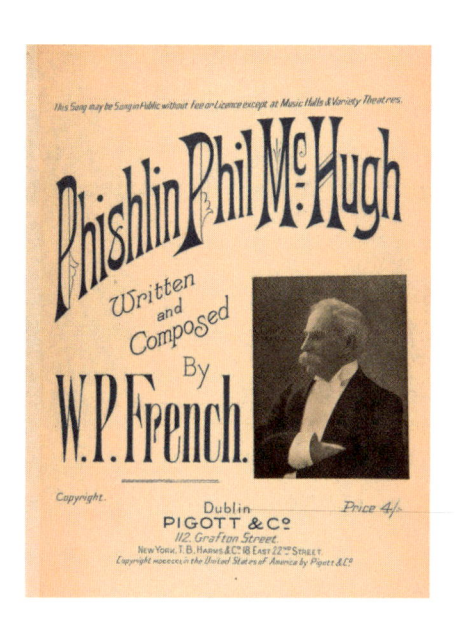

Song cover 'Phishlin Phil McHugh'
Percy French Collection North Down Museum

The children's song, 'The Hoodoo' came from *Noah's Ark*, a children's play written by French and Brendan Stewert (music by Collisson and J. St A. Johnson), which ran at the Waldorf Theatre, London, in 1906. There were also some rather less straightforward musical compositions at this energetic and creative time. Apart from the already mentioned *Noah's Ark*, French wrote the children's operetta *Freda and the Fairies* (music by Caroline Maude), *The Kerry Courting*, a comedy song-cycle about matchmaking in Ireland, and a song cyclette, *Bad Ballads for Baddish Babies*.

As an indication of French's growing status both as entertainer and celebrity, we find him amongst the 'celebrity' guests of the owner of Glenveagh Castle in Co. Donegal in August 1909. Also present was his long time colleague, Eddy Radcliffe with his wife May. Eddy Radcliffe was indeed a special friend as is reflected in a verse tribute 'To E.R':

For once you heard the fairy bells,
And saw the little shehogues play,
And knew at last the magic spells
That lead the lover to Glenveagh.

Oh Poet, when the touch of Time
Has turned those auburn locks to grey,
Still may the bells of Faerie chime
That once re-echoed round Glenveagh.

These magic spells must have been working on French himself. In praise of that beautiful spot he also composed an unusual form of verse, a triolet:

When you get to Glenveagh
You have no wish to leave it,
The lake you portray
When you get to Glenveagh,
"Your car sir" they say
But you cannot perceive it,
You've got to Glenveagh
And you hardly can leave it.

It was here too that French memorably penned a kind of epitaph in the visitor's book:

Remember me is all I ask,
And yet
If the remembrance prove a task
Forget.

Far right:
Page from visitors'
book, Glenveagh
Castle, Co. Donegal

Courtesy of
Glenveagh Castle

Triolet.

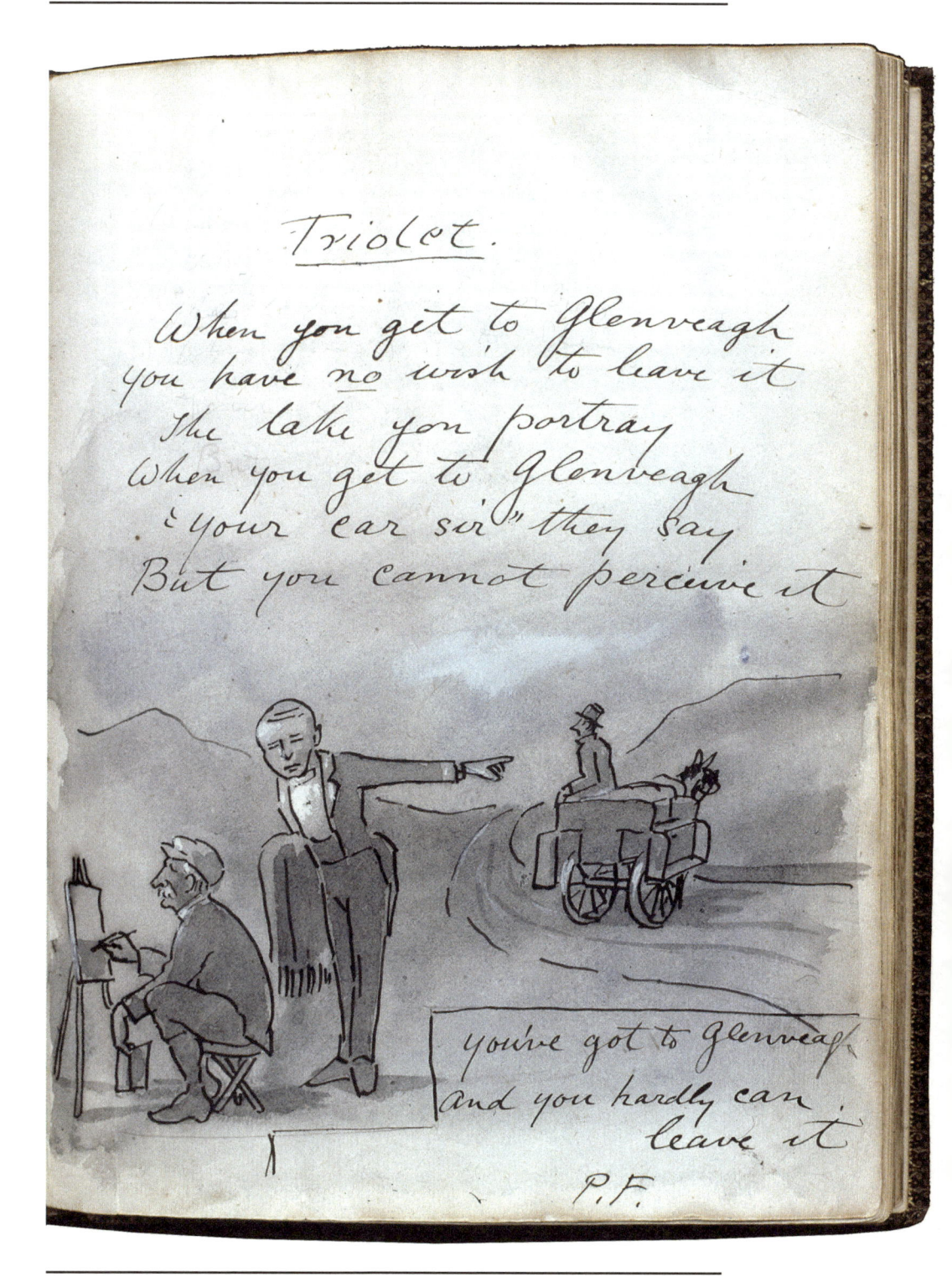

When you get to Glenveagh
You have no wish to leave it
The lake you portray
When you get to Glenveagh
"Your car sir" they say
But you cannot perceive it
You've got to Glenveagh
And you hardly can leave it

P.F.

21. CELESTIAL PAINTING

One might be forgiven for thinking that there was little time or energy remaining for developing a secondary income from his watercolour art. However, we know that French held an exhibition in Manchester and another at the Modern Gallery, London in 1903. It is also understood that the Marchioness of Londonderry commissioned French to depict the places visited by King Edward and Queen Alexandra on their tour to Ireland in 1903. Although it is not possible to say with certainty whether he completed the project, at least one painting by Percy French relating to a 'Touring Exhibition' of such work surfaced some years ago. There were occasional entries in his engagement diaries for painting expeditions to scenic locations like Anglesey.

'Mountstewart', the home of the Marchioness of Londonderry, Co. Down

Watercolour by Percy French

Percy French Collection North Down Museum

Then came a major turning point of this aspect of his career. He made the important discovery that a special 'English' commercial value was attached to what he called his 'bog picture.' His daughter Ettie writes of him painting 'hard' in Devon and Hampshire and exhibiting his work in cities such as Leeds and Liverpool, but 'the first choice of buyers was invariably a bog picture, which led later to his repeating himself, over and over again, in pot-boiling bog sketches'. Sometimes, to fulfil the London buyers' romantic vision of Ireland, he was requested to add a thatched cottage or two (or even a red-skirted Irish colleen) to an already completed picture. Never a purist and ever willing to comply with market forces, French could insert a cottage precariously perched beside a boghole!

A bog picture with cottage and red-skirted colleen

Watercolour by Percy French

Courtesy of Co. Roscommon Percy French Society

Of course there was more to each bog picture than the bog. It was really the sky that made them especially evocative. Even to the present day, and despite the fact that an apparently inexhaustible number keep reaching the market, French's depictions of rainy skies over mountain and bog remain in greatest demand in the auction houses of London, Belfast and Dublin. He exhibited with the Irish watercolourists, Mildred Anne Butler, Bingham McGuinness and Claude Hayes at London's New Dudley Gallery in 1907. Interestingly, joint exhibition with Richard Orpen R.H.A. at the New Dudley Gallery in 1909 was themed 'The Pageant of the Sky'. It is worth recalling here that it had been the skies over Cavan that were the early exciting focus for his love of the art of watercolour painting.

'The Pageant of the Sky'
Exhibition catalogue, New Dudley Gallery, London, 1909
Percy French Collection North Down Museum

Celestial Painting (Sunset at Renvyle)

When painters leave this world, we grieve
For the hand that will work no more,
But who can say that they rest alway
On that still celestial shore?

No! No! they choose from the rainbow hues,
And winging from Paradise,
They come to paint, now bold, now faint,
The tones of our sunset skies.

When I see them there I can almost swear
That grey is from Whistler's brain!
That crimson flush was Turner's brush!
And the gold is Claude Lorraine.

The End of the Holiday

Fold up the box, the wind is chill,
The hills are turning grey.
Tomorrow I must pay my bill
And speed me far away -
Back to the world again - but still
Thank God for such a day!

22. SMOKE PAINTING AND OTHER UNUSUAL ARTISTIC SKILLS

A lesser-known example of Percy French's extraordinary flair as an artist was his skill at what is known as 'smoke painting'. In her Foreword to *The Irish Troubador: Songs of Percy French*, his daughter Ettie mentions that his most original artistic entertainment was the smoke picture which 'could not be done on the stage, but was very popular at dinners'. All he needed was a lighted candle, the back of a plate which he passed to and fro at different heights above the flame, and a match.' The flame caused smudges on the glazed surface of the white dinner plate and a black and white sketch was then etched on using the sharpened end of the match.

Smoke plate
Percy French
Collection North Down Museum

Unsuitable for the stage, this unusual artistic talent hardly added much to what French called his exchequer, but it made him a popular dinner guest for the society hostess. One story tells of how one such lady lost most of her best dinner service as each of her guests left with a special souvenir. Brendan O'Dowda refers to a letter from the Prince of Wales thanking him for his gift of a book of watercolours and 'the plate'. One wonders if he painted it on location on a piece of Royal china. Mrs De Burgh Daly mentions that specimens were left at both the universities of Oxford and Cambridge.

French himself wrote at the time that smoke pictures had been perfected by German artists whose works commanded high prices in that country, but the British public were a little doubtful as to the precise place of 'this curious medium among the decorative arts'. According to French, pouring a kind of varnish known as 'Soehnee Freres' over it could preserve the picture. However, despite such preservation techniques, the fragile nature of the basic ingredient probably explains why few good examples survive today.

As already noted, Percy French as writer and entertainer tended not to take matters at face value or at first impression. One can perhaps also apply this characteristic to his approach to drawing and sketching. He had an ability to draw ambidextrously, producing certain outlines simultaneously with both hands, something, he casually explained, that 'was not hard to do, as you have only to think with the right hand and the left will perform the same curves automatically.' Likewise, an ability to see things upside down extended his variety of stage entertainments to include comic line drawings and colourful landscapes in chalk. These would begin as one image and be turned on their heads, ending as something quite different. Indeed it was his drawing skills that distinguished French's shows from many others.

'Jungfrau'
Watercolour by Percy French
Percy French Society Archive

23. 'ACROSS THE ATLANTICAL SEA'

Towards the end of this busy Edwardian decade, Dr Collisson, then recovered from a breakdown suffered some years earlier, rejoined French in his regular recitals at London's Steinway Hall for 'Six Grand Matinees'. A *Daily Telegraph* review of a French and Collisson performance in April 1910 was entirely positive: 'The house was sold out and joy was triumphant, as indeed it had to be.' Their sophisticated 'Humours of Art and Music' show by the 'painter and the pianist' clearly impressed critics. It resulted in an engagement from the impresario J.C. Duff that took them to Canada, USA, Bermuda, West Indies, and Panama. This had to be the apogee of French's career as an entertainer, as is suggested by the jaunty, arms akimbo photograph of him attired in a lightweight suit for the warmer climes. 'We unite brains, beauty, brushwork and banjos in one harmonic whole' the duo proclaimed confidently.

Ready for the tropics
Percy French Collection North Down Museum

'Humours of Art and Music'
French and Collisson ready for their American Tour
Percy French Collection North Down Museum

Their departure was celebrated by friends at the Savage Club in London with a special farewell dinner. The occasion was also marked by the presentation of a caricature of the performers by the artist Phil May. At Paddington station French's sister Mrs De Burgh Daly joined Lennie, the three girls and many other friends, artists and musicians to wish them good luck and bon voyage. Two saffron-kilted Irish pipers added further colour to a memorable occasion as French and his friend Collisson began their adventure by Allan liner across the Atlantic, or the 'Atlantical Sea', as it is described in French's famous song about the West Clare Railway. His mostly sad but partially humorous monologue poem 'An Emigrant's Letter' (later put to music by Ernest Hastings, a well-known London performer of comic material) is inspired by a young emigrant's remark that French overheard by chance aboard the liner as 'the waves hid the last bit of ould Donegal'. There is a wealth of understated sadness in the young man's realisation of what he is leaving behind, 'Where they're cuttin' the corn in Creesla the day.'

'Bon Voyage' from the members of London's Savage Club

Drawing by Phil May

Percy French Collection North Down Museum

'Across the Atlantical Sea' 119

It was a time when all evidence, including amusing and informative letters to Lennie and the family, suggested that French was enjoying the view from the peak of his professional career. Indeed, these letters, colourfully and wittily composed while in holiday mood, are as superbly written as any of his other literary activities. For perhaps the first and only time in his life he was off the treadmill and able to relax and enjoy the luxury of first-class travel on board the liner.

French's family composing a letter to him, Christmas 1910

Percy French Collection North Down Museum

He makes light of a heavy storm that had Dr Collisson suffering the agonies of sea-sickness. He entertained the crew and passengers during the ship's concert by singing 'My Old Kentucky Home' and 'Oft in the Stilly Night'. Then with a Steinway Grand on board, he and Collisson, perhaps influenced by Bleriot's crossing of the English Channel by airplane a few months earlier, set to work on a new song called 'Flanagan's Flying Machine'. Icebergs observed glistening on the horizon added something picturesque for French's ready watercolour brush. The Titanic disaster was yet to happen; maybe Collisson's fear of their ship 'toppling over' in the storm was somewhat prophetic in concept.

'Icebergs'
Watercolour by Percy French
Percy French Collection North Down Museum

Differing personality types became evident in Montréal, where the ebullient Collisson couldn't wait to see the city sights while the more reflective French was more interested in the banks of the St Lawrence river 'with the morning sun shining on the red and gold of the maples and the little French cottages dotted along'. They entertained and were themselves entertained, feted, and given a good press as they moved through Montréal, Kingston, Toronto (Massey Hall) and Niagara.

In Kingston they were 'taken for a ride' in every sense by 'Hungry Hank the Hackman'. The luxury of a fine hotel in Boston was much appreciated by French – a contrast, one supposes, to one of his experiences back home 'by the salt say water'. The incident is immortalised in his song, 'Mick's Hotel': 'What the devil do ye want with a bedroom bell. Haven't you a voice! and can't you yell.'

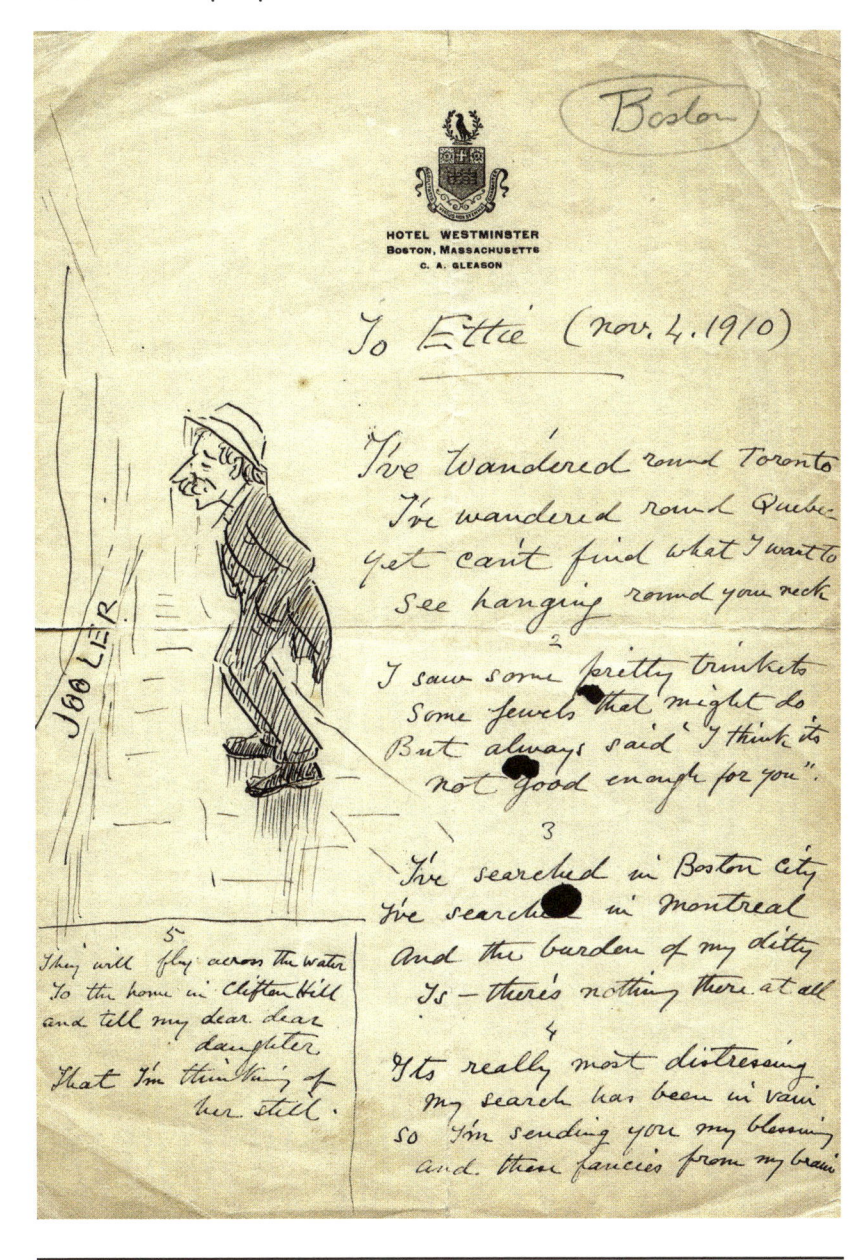

A letter from Boston

Percy French Collection North Down Museum

Having played in the Mendelssohn Hall and fulfilled various engagements in New York, the friends sail for Bermuda. French, the artist, notices on their approach: 'islands dotted with mushrooms apparently, which turned out to be bungalows, walled and roofed with slabs of snow white coral, their green shutters and wooden balconies reflected in blue and emerald lagoons'.

'New York from the Hudson'

Watercolour by Percy French

Percy French Collection North Down Museum

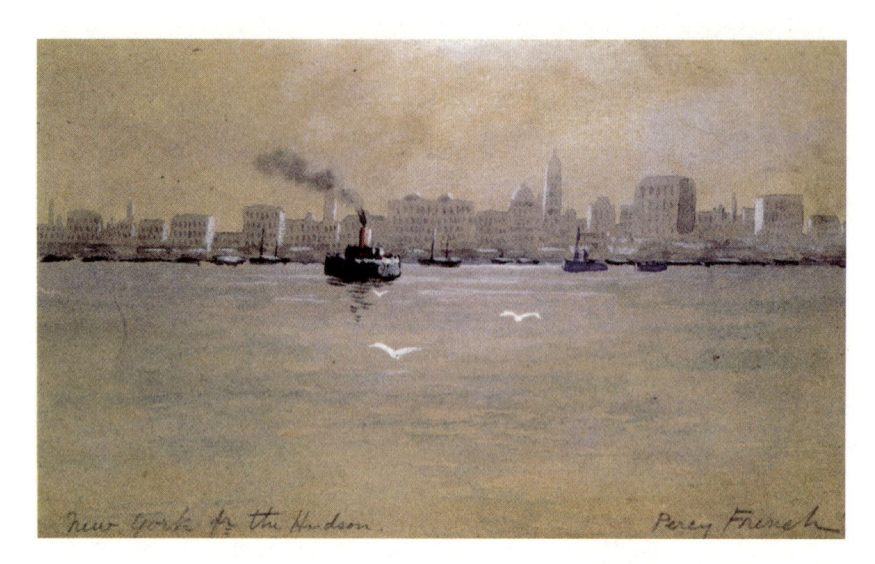

The letters J.F. carved on rocks in memory of Juan Fernandez, who discovered the islands, reminded French of his youngest daughter, Joan. He mentions it in a letter and drawing sent to her. Next is Jamaica, where 'the blue mountains are an everlasting joy and make a beautiful background for the Bougainvillea and the Lignum Vitae':

>*Oh the old Jamaica days!*
>*When the sun's mid-winter rays*
>*Have failed to pierce the fogs that fill*
>*Our murky alleyways.*
>
>*We'll sit beside the fire, old friend,*
>*And as the embers blaze*
>*Go rafting down the Rio*
>*In the old Jamaica days.*

'West Indian Party'
Watercolour by Percy French
Percy French Collection North Down Museum

French and Collisson sailed on to Trinidad where they were quarantined for a time. French describes, with a touch of irony, 'the sight of us all sitting round the room with thermometers sticking out of our mouths is very attractive.' In Panama their proposed shows had not been organized so it was all play and no work for 'Duffs Dinky Dudelets and Drawing-room Dissipators of Gloom' until, after a six-month tour, it was 'Hurrah for the homeward bound.'

'Girl in Canoe'
Watercolour by Percy French
Percy French Collection North Down Museum

Chelsea Palace programme
Percy French Collection North Down Museum

The engagement diary kept by Lennie notes for Easter Monday, 17 April 1911, 'Willie arrives at Southampton.' On 28 April 'W.' goes to Dublin to perform at the Abbey Theatre (*Tales from my Tour Book*) before the Steinway Hall beckons again for 'Mr Percy French and Dr Houston Collisson.' Their material, now including 'Flanagan's Flying Machine', is influenced by their American experiences and receives enthusiastic press reviews. A musical fantasy *A Frog He Would*, from a book by Percy French, ran for a week at Chelsea Palace Theatre.

In 1912 'That's why we're Burying Him' was initially written to fit a Collisson tune and, not too surprisingly, was a cause of disagreement between the friends. French's daughter, Ettie, eventually wrote the music. Whilst the lyrics are clever, the overall impact is not especially memorable. With an amusingly anti-heroic theme, reminiscent of 'Jim Wheelahan's Automobeel' and 'Maguire's Motorbike', its mock-sad chorus might make it particularly suitable for music hall entertainment.

At this time a letter from French to daughter Ettie on her eighteenth birthday enclosed 'something to buy a memento of the day ... this is all that can be found in the wallet of stoneybroke the strolling singer.' It is understood that he had been defrauded of the financial rewards of the American tour.

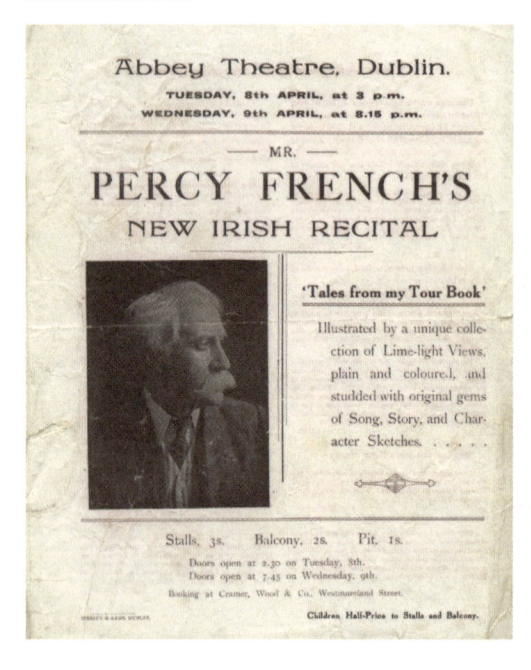

Abbey Theatre programme
Percy French Collection North Down Museum

24. 'TONES THAT ARE TENDER AND TONES THAT ARE GRUFF'

From 'Come Back, Paddy Reilly to Ballyjamesduff'
by Percy French

There are many and varied stories about how one of Percy French's best loved songs came to be written, but there is little doubt that the central character was a real person who drove a sidecar for a living. It is likely that Paddy Reilly had provided transport for Percy French during his days in Cavan as an engineer in the 1880s and that some thirty years later French discovered that his old friend was no longer around. It is generally understood that Paddy Reilly had departed from Ireland for Scotland in something of a hurry; his horse and car were discovered tied to a post in the town of Oldcastle.

The songwriter imagines the feelings and memories of the now 'toil-worn and tough' Paddy Reilly, puffing on his dudeen (stump of a pipe) and reflecting nostalgically on his hometown (the Garden of Eden has not vanished after all!) and the love of his life, Rosie Kilrain. There is a beautifully expressed sense of place: 'Just turn to the left at the bridge of Finea and stop when halfway to Cootehill'. There is a musicality in these unpretentious words. However, despite the overall sentimental ambience, as is his wont Percy French does not avoid the harder side of life. He softens it with an element of understated humour; in this case, an altercation after a dance and someone 'slanderin' Rosie Kilrain' leads Paddy to recall 'the day that I took Long Magee by the scruff and assisted him into a drain'.

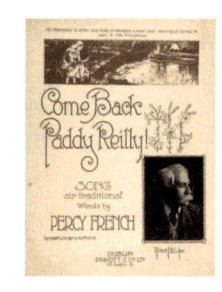

Song cover 'Come Back, Paddy Reilly'
Percy French Collection North Down Museum

Yet again this tribute to an old friend is not quite a comic song. It is more a lament for lost times of youth is maybe somewhat reflective of French's own sense of the passing years and of friendships that will never be renewed. As with most of French's work, underlying sentiments of poignancy and regret are flavoured with humour and human understanding that resonate to an extent in all our lives.

As with all songs, the ultimate success of these songs is based on the melding of words with an appropriate air. This talent is surely another of Percy French's strengths. In this case there is a pleasantly plaintive feeling engendered by the melody of 'Come Back, Paddy Reilly', one that has been featured in scenarios varying from that most Gaelic of occasions, an all-Ireland Hurling final at Dublin's Croke Park, to the most English of traditional pageantry, when the band of the Regiment of the Irish Guards played an Irish medley featuring 'Come Back, Paddy Reilly' and 'Slattery's Mounted Fut' while Trooping the Colour at London's Horse Guards Parade on the Queen's birthday.

A visit to Ballyjamesduff some years ago revealed that Paddy Reilly did indeed come back to his native town, his name is engraved amongst other family ones in the local cemetery. Meanwhile an excellent bronze of Percy French is seated in the town square, looking down that street as he imagined his friend 'on the very first morn.'

Bronze of Percy French in Ballyjamesduff
Courtesy of Cavan County Museum

25. 'HE LOVED THE OLD COUNTRY AND ITS PEOPLE'

Mr H. Franklin

Although Percy French quickly resumed normal professional engagements upon his return from his American tour, it is likely that the Edwardian world of opulent private entertaining and the role of the society entertainer was in decline. Whatever the reason, in 1911 French's annual tour of Ireland extended from 1 August until the first week of October. Loughrea, Glaslough and Portsalon are among the less familiar performance locations. The length and intensity of his Irish tours continued to increase. In April 1912 he paid a short visit to Ireland before undertaking an even longer unbroken period of Irish engagements from August all the way to mid-November.

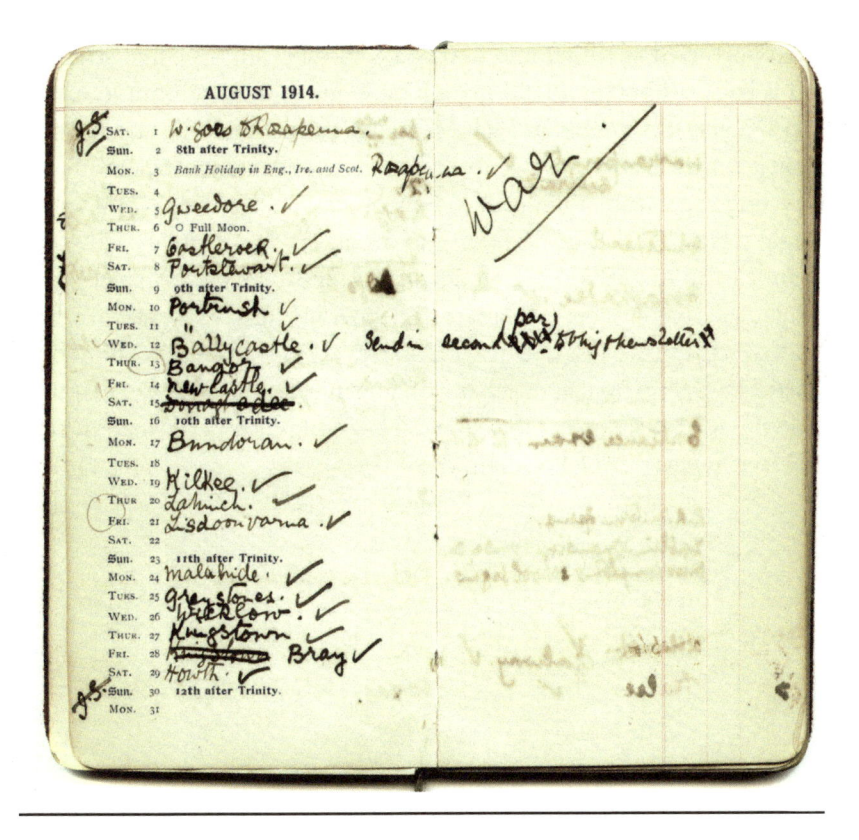

Page from engagement diary, August 1914

Percy French Collection North Down Museum

The outbreak of war in 1914, as French's daughter has written, 'was a mortal blow' to her father's career in London, where the social side of life gave way to the grim realities of warfare. The big houses became convalescent homes for the injured and inevitably available money was directed to the war effort. It was of course different in Ireland, where he seemed to have a never-ending source of engagements throughout the length and breadth of the country. It meant more and more travelling both within Ireland and also to and from his home in England. What are described as the 'Franklin's Tours' had already added the midland towns of Ireland to the seaside venues that had been the traditional focus of his summer activities. These are perhaps the times that survive most colourfully and fondly in Irish folk memory and that earned him his almost legendary status as the 'Irish Troubadour'. His one-man entertainments touched almost every town in Ireland.

That French should undertake such itineraries can only be explained by the comprehensive coverage of the Irish railway system of that time. Without such an extraordinarily countrywide transport system, the story of Percy French would surely be different. Now, a century later, he is often portrayed as riding into town on a bicycle with his banjo strapped to his back. Although he did use a bicycle in earlier days around Cavan and Dublin, this quaint and lovable image cannot at all be sustained in reality. Evidence points to twenty or more engagements in one month and bicycling to get from Ballinrobe to Bangor via Waterford and Cork would surely relegate the Tour de France to an outing for amateur sightseers! From 1 to 30 August 1912 the following twenty-three performances were scheduled: Ballinasloe, Mullingar, Edenderry, Naas, Roscrea, Carlow, Waterford, Ennis, Cork, a private party, Wexford, Dublin, Limerick, Castleblayney, Armagh, Strabane, Dungannon, Limavady, Coleraine, Ballymoney, Portadown, Cookstown, Newry! French performed in over 180 Irish towns during his lifetime.

In his book *Irish Railways: A New History*, Tom Ferris writes that the 'Golden Age of Ireland's Railways' was between 1880 and 1914, an era that obviously coincides very much with the height of Percy French's career as an entertainer. Likewise, a 2014 RTÉ television production entitled 'Building Ireland' mentioned, 'between 1850 and 1950 Ireland had a love affair with the railways.' It is understood that Ireland enjoyed the densest network of railways in the world at that time. In a sense the railways transformed the country and were the main reflection of the Industrial Revolution. Some extraordinary feats of engineering were accomplished during those years.

Facilitated by the railways, tourism was an important business opportunity in the late nineteenth century. In line with the extension of the Belfast and County Down Railway to Newcastle, the company also built the majestic Slieve Donard Hotel in the place where, in the words of French's unforgettable song, 'The Mountains o' Mourne sweep down to the sea.' Today, in the foyer of the still-flourishing hotel a wall plaque proudly commemorates a visit by Percy French on 20 September 1915 when he was a guest of the manager 'without payment' (a gesture that was surely appreciated by the entertainer whose income, we have already noted, had been so negatively affected by the outbreak of war in 1914). Indeed the entertainer's name is almost synonymous with the seaside town of Newcastle. A well-known restaurant in the town is called 'The Percy French'. Along the well-designed promenade, the image of Percy French is etched in stainless steel against the background of the mountains, whose beauty he in turn had etched on the world of music and song.

On tour with Lennie
Percy French Collection North Down Museum

The main railway lines were supplemented by a variety of narrow gauge systems. Though French made the West Clare Railway the most famous, Mr H. Franklin of Sligo, who organized French's extended tours in Ireland, mentions the 'ingenious invention' of the Ballybunion to Listowel railway: 'There is only one rail and the two compartments are built quite near the ground, just like two creels of turf on a donkey's back, the back of the ass being the rail.' He and Percy French were asked by the guard to change sides to balance some other passengers! We might regard this as another quaint Percy French anecdote (tell a good one while you're at it!) until we realise that the Ballybunion to Listowel railway was one of the first monorail systems ever to be used. Devised by a French engineer, Charles Lartigue, it opened in 1888 and was closed in 1924 'due to Civil War damage'. Nowadays monorails constitute the main transport facilities in such diverse and sophisticated cities as Moscow and Las Vegas.

Letter from Ballybunion

Percy French Collection North Down Museum

On another of French's visits to Kerry an overworked horse eventually refused to continue pulling the car. A man with his turf cart befriended them and they entered Ballybunion in procession with the owner walking ahead with a lantern, their luggage and banjo on top of the turf and French and Franklin bringing up the rear. French's daughter has written of how Franklin did more to help her father in all sorts of ways than can be recorded. The two friends travelled quite a lot together and Franklin has recounted how French, whose 'brush was never idle', would often sketch all day before a performance. In Franklin's own words:

> Mr French's views on the important topics of the day were always broadminded and tolerant, and of course he could hardly escape adding a spice of humour even to the saddest theme. He loved the old country and its people, and he was happiest when he was sketching the lovely sunsets at Bundoran, the Mayo bogs, the Connemara Mountains and many other beautiful spots around the Emerald Isle.

Mr Franklin also refers to French's famous monologue/recitation/sketch, 'The Four Farrellys', which was then, as it is now, a prime favourite of audiences and lovers of the works of Percy French. French most likely wrote it during his early days in London, when a name in a hotel register set off memories of identically named but widely different individuals and attitudes from the four corners of Ireland. It is yet another illustration of how his thoughts tended to turn to the people, the places, the problems and even the politics of Ireland. From an entertainer's viewpoint, it provides opportunities for four distinct characterisations. With a mixture of humour and pathos it imparts a sense of an Irishness capable of diversity but, as we now know, not politically sustainable.

Percy French (see illustration)

Self-signed caricature from the visitors' book at the Abercorn Arms, Newtownstewart, where he stayed from 26 May to 2 June 1914

Printed in the Tyrone Constitution, *July 1999*

The Four Farrellys

In a small hotel in London I was sitting down to dine,
When the waiter brought the register and asked me if I'd sign,
And as I signed I saw a name that set my heart astir –
A certain 'Francis Farrelly' had signed the register.
I knew a lot of Farrellys and out of all the crew
I kept on 'sort of wonderin' which Farrelly were you.
And when I'd finished dinner I sat back in my chair,
Going round my native land to find, what Farrelly you were.

South

Were you the keen-eyed Kerryman I met below Kenmare,
Who told me that when Ireland fought 'the odds were never fair,'
If Cromwell had met Sarsfield, or met Owen Roe O'Neill,
It's not to Misther Gladstone we'd be lookin' for repeal.
Would have Ireland for the Irish, not a Saxon to be seen,
And only Gaelic spoken in that House in College Green.
Told me landlords wor the Divil! their agents ten times worse,
And iv'ry sort of government for Ireland was a curse!
Oh! if you're that Francis Farrelly, your dreams have not come true,
Still, Slainthe! Slainthe! Fransheen! for I like a man like you!

North

Or were you the Francis Farrelly that often used to say
He'd like to blow them Papishes from Darry walls away?
The boy who used to bother me that Orange Lodge to join,
And thought that history started with the Battle o' the Boyne,–
I was not all with ye, Francis, the Pope is not ma friend,
But still I hope, poor man, he'll die without that bloody end,–
And when yer quit from care yerself, and get to Kingdom Come,
It's no use teachin' you the harp – you'll play the Orange drum!
Och! man, ye wor a fighter, of that I had no doubt,
For I seen ye in Belfast one night when the Antrim Road was out!
And many a time that evenin' I thought that ye wor dead,
The way them Papish pavin' stones was hoppin' off yer head.
Oh! if you're that Francis Farrelly who came from North Tyrone –
Here's lookin' to ye, Francis, but do leave the Pope alone!

East

Or were you the Francis Farrelly that in my college days
For strolling on the Kingstown Pier had such a curious craze?
D'ye mind them lovely sisters – the blonde and the brunette?
I know I've not forgotten, and I don't think you forget!
That picnic at the Dargle – and the other at the Scalp –
How my heart was palpitatin' – hers wasn't – not a palp!
Someone said ye married money – and maybe you were wise,
But the gold you loved was in her hair, and the diamonds in her eyes!
So I like to think ye married her and that you're with her yet,
'Twas some 'meleesha' officer that married the brunette;
But the blonde one always loved ye, and I knew you loved her too,
So me blessin's on ye, Francis, and the blue sky over you!

West

Or were you the Francis Farrelly I met so long ago,
In the bog below Belmullet, in the County of Mayo?
That long-legged, freckled Francis with the deep-set wistful eyes,
That seemed to take their colour from those ever-changing skies.
That put his flute together as I sketched the distant scene,
And played me 'Planxty Kelly' and the 'Wakes of Inniskeen'.
That told me in the Autumn he'd be sailin' to the West,
To try and make his fortune and send money to the rest.
And would I draw a picture of the place where he was born,
And he'd hang it up, and look at it, and not feel so forlorn.
And when I had it finished, you got up from where you sat,
And you said, 'Well, you're the Divil, and I can't say more than that.'
Oh! if you're that Francis Farrelly, your fortune may be small,
But I'm thinking – thinking – Francis, that I love you best of all;
And I never can forget you – though it's years and years ago –
In the bog below Belmullet, in the County of Mayo.

26. OH SWITZERLAND!

Early in 1914 Percy French toured the Swiss winter sporting resorts with Captain Brandreth Gibbs. The six-week tour was in aid of the 'Waifs and Strays', a charity for which Dr Collisson and Gibbs worked assiduously. It was an opportunity for him to enjoy travelling around Switzerland with Gibbs doing all the worrying about trains, travel times and misplaced tickets. He wrote regularly to wife Lennie in a light-hearted and humorous vein, always with colourful observations of the characters and scenery that excited his interest. French the artist found Lucerne grey and uninteresting in winter light. Thence to Engelberg which he reached on the electric railway 'through a double row of Christmas trees and snow covered chalets – until the command, "tout le monde descende!"' He gave his first show at the Grand Hotel to a large and appreciative audience and they donned fancy dress for the ball on New Year's Eve.

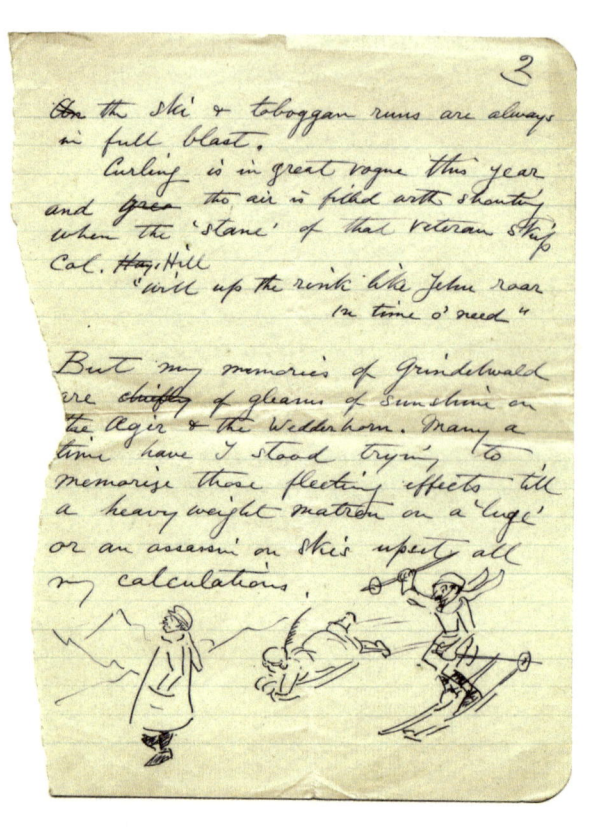

Part of a letter to his wife, Lennie, from Switzerland

Percy French Collection North Down Museum

French also enjoyed other well-known sport centres such as Davos, Klosters and St. Moritz-Dorf-Engadin. He colourfully described them in his letters to Lennie. 'The chatter and laughter in the lounges of a morning is so incessant', he wrote, that it was an inspiration for a rhyme:

> *There's German in the music room,*
> *There's French upon the stair,*
> *There's English in the Grand Salon,*
> *There's laughter everywhere.*
> *The bunch from Boston hold their own*
> *At every sort of noise,*
> *Oh, Switzerland! Oh, Switzerland!*
> *The land for healthy boys!*

Percy French is known to have stated that Switzerland was the only country, apart from Ireland, that he really wished to paint. His watercolour depictions of the vivid sunset glow against the cold effect of the snow-clad mountains in Switzerland are especially skilful. French himself regarded these Swiss watercolours as some of his best. Ironically, these Alpine scenes did not sell as profitably at home as did his Irish rainy skies and bog scenes, which collectors apparently identified as the real Percy French. It does seem that French's reputation as a watercolourist is often judged, not always for the better, by his commercial success with the 'bog painting' which he trotted out in varying degrees of skill and concentration, either to please the customer or to help with his never overflowing exchequer.

'Alpine Slopes'
Watercolour by Percy French
Percy French Collection North Down Museum

'Alpine Glow'
Watercolour by Percy French
Percy French Collection North Down Museum

Inevitably, he was intrigued with the snow-clad Jungfrau Mountain. From certain angles it looks like the face of a young girl in repose and French, not surprisingly for one who could draw 'up-side-down' on the platform, painted the scene in its various moods. From time to time examples of his Swiss paintings reach the auction houses but fetch only perhaps half the price of his traditional 'pot boilers'. In 1986 UNICEF chose one of his paintings 'Celerina' as a suitable image for its Christmas card.

It is understood that Percy French had planned to return to Switzerland and paint many more pictures there but was prevented from doing so by the outbreak of the Great War. He applied for a passport in December 1919 in order to accompany Dr Collisson to Switzerland to raise funds for the Royal Surgical Aid Society. Owing to failing health he was destined not to enjoy the 'Alpine glow' again.

'Swiss Cottage'
Watercolour by Percy French
Percy French Collection North Down Museum

27. THE CHANGING SCENE

French published his final song in 1915. 'Larry Mick McGarry', with its bouncy toe-tapping lilt, is yet another tale of life's lessons and another example of French undermining affected airs and graces. In this case the suave Larry fancies himself as an assured ladies' man; he toys with the affections of girls who fall for his beguiling and superior style, for the time being anyway:

> *Oh! Larry played old Harry*
> *With the girls about the place,*
> *At the dancin' they'd be glancin'*
> *At the features of his face,*
> *But he never would endeavour*
> *To be lover-like until*
> *Mary Carey, she' a fairy,*
> *Had him goin' like a mill.*

It was a time when French began to work with the help of a female partner. At a dinner in Dublin's United Arts Club he had discovered Florence Marks who, without knowing French was present, earned 'tumultuous applause' for her rendition of his song 'Phil the Fluter's Ball'. He was impressed. Subsequently she wrote that she had the privilege and pleasure of helping French in public performances for about a year.

Betty Duncan replaced Florence, who was unable to travel with him. On 2 October 1915 the *Tuam Herald* advertised 'Mr Percy French and Miss Betty Duncan on tour with Humours of Ireland at the Town Hall.' Subsequently, he was joined by May Laffan, an actress with a 'delightful soprano voice' who played the banjo with a virtuosity equal to his own. The assistance of a female partner enabled French to include beautifully characterized sketches or short plays such as *The Letter from the Front* or *Michael O'Ryan Gets the Pension* in his programmes. The latter is a mildly satirical and philosophical look at the introduction of the old age pension to Ireland when, as the story goes, some 130 per cent of those considered eligible successfully applied!

An engagement with Florence Marks
Percy French Collection North Down Museum

*Drawing by
Kitty Lloyd*
*Percy French
Collection North
Down Museum*

Betty Duncan was the daughter of Jim and Ellie Duncan, who were long-time friends of Percy French and his wife Lennie. They were deeply involved in the arts scene in Dublin. Patricia Boylan, in her history of the United Arts Club, *All Cultivated People*, mentions that Ellie Duncan sent out the circular letter that led to the Club's foundation. She elicited support from writers such as George Bernard Shaw, W.B. Yeats, Lady Gregory and Percy French. In 1914 guests at a house dinner there were delighted with Percy French's 'Tales from my Town'. In April 1915 he held an exhibition of his paintings at the Club, where he often stayed when in Dublin.

In its 'Between the Acts' column, the *Irish Life* magazine of 1 October 1915 mentions a recital called 'Lights and Shadows of Irish Life' by 'Mr Percy French and Miss Betty Duncan'. It continued,

> And now Ireland is glad to hear that the man who has been for many years the fountain-head of so much wholesome fun has not been forgotten amid this time of stress, for the government have granted him an annuity which will go far to tide him over the troubled waters. Long may he live to enjoy this well-timed gift, for few men have given their services more freely in the cause of charity than he.

Apart from alleviating financial pressures, it must have been a source of unstated satisfaction to him to be awarded a pension from the Civil List, like W.B. Yeats.

*Percy French with
Betty Duncan*
*Percy French
Collection North
Down Museum*

28. THE CHALLENGES OF WARTIME

By 1916 the War had only intensified and Percy French needed to spend more and more of his time in Ireland. Early in the year he wrote and produced a revue-style show called *How Dublin Does It*. With mostly new material, this 'Typical, Topical, Part Philanthropical Talk of the Times' ran for a week at the Little Theatre, Sackville Street (as it was then known) in Dublin. It had a cast of four performers plus himself. One was his daughter Ettie French (sometimes 'Ettie Percy French') and another was Betty Duncan. An old playbill shows another performance of the revue at Blackrock Town Hall on 23 February. Amongst the characters to be played (satirized?) by Percy French himself was the poet W.B. Yeats. It would have been more than interesting to see how French presented the poet, as they were surely at opposite ends of the literary and philosophical spectrum.

The 1916 Rebellion in Ireland made a planned staging in Eastbourne of the same revue untenable. Mrs De Burgh Daly writes that Percy French's heart was in Ireland, even during the height of his popularity when he was entertaining either in private houses or delighting distinguished audiences at the Steinway Hall in London. The troubled state of Ireland would undoubtedly have been upsetting for him, very likely causing him, as Brendan O'Dowda has written, 'a deep, deep sadness'. However, despite a hiatus of some months, the indefatigable entertainer was determined to continue with his annual Irish tour, a hugely demanding schedule lasting from August into November of that fateful year.

Despite all the changes wrought to his pre-war programme of engagements, the schools and colleges continued to avail themselves of French's intimate style of entertainment. A tribute from L.A.G. Strong of Brighton College is worth repeating:

> Prince of our entertainers, best loved, was Percy French. Old now and frail, with a mane of white hair and a drooping moustache, he insisted on arriving early and having tea in the School House with the boys.

Those lucky enough to be at the chosen table would be entertained with all manners of stories, card tricks, and strange beasts made from napkins and newspapers. Two or three would receive landscapes executed in candle-smoke on plate or saucer, and fixed with a kind of varnish, which they would gladly purchase from the school and treasure in their studies. Then, his vitality heightened, the old man would mount the platform in the gym, and give the most versatile single entertainment I have seen from anyone but Danny Kaye. He would sing in a sweet small tenor voice, accompanying himself on the guitar. He would paint a landscape on a large sheet of paper draped over a blackboard, telling stories all the time, then turn it upside down and reveal it as something entirely different. The applause commanded by Percy French rang louder and longer than anyone else's and I, who had heard him also in Ireland, felt a thrill of national pride.

For further engagements, however, he had to widen his horizons and looked towards the variety stage. The *Daily Mirror* of 12 July 1916 advertised 'Mr Percy French – his first appearance on the variety stage – this week at the Putney Hippodrome.' He also did a short session at the Coliseum Music Hall, but the nature of the bigger stage demanded too much of his ageing voice (none of our modern amplification in those days) and the audience also expected a different style of entertainment. The song cycle 'The Kerry Courting', written by himself and Collisson, was staged in a revue featuring well-known artists Stanley Holloway and Patricia Burke.

The Stage Society honoured him with a deserved special lunch. But it was also the time when his health began to fail. This was signalled by a serious injury received from a fall in his own house. He had barely recovered before suffering a further accident in Blackrock, Co. Dublin, when jumping onto a moving train on his way for a performance in Bray. According to his sister, French was never the same again, although he resolutely refused to abandon any engagements.

Mrs De Burgh Daly records that, as with most of his work at that time, a percentage of French's takings went to the Red Cross charity, whose work was so vital at wartime. Back in London with Collisson he became more involved in such wartime charity work.

James N. Healy notes in *Percy French and His Songs* that owing to a heavy air raid they were the only artists who turned up to perform for a London Catholic Bazaar. Instead of performing their scheduled two items they stayed on and gave a full two-hour show throughout the worst of the air raid.

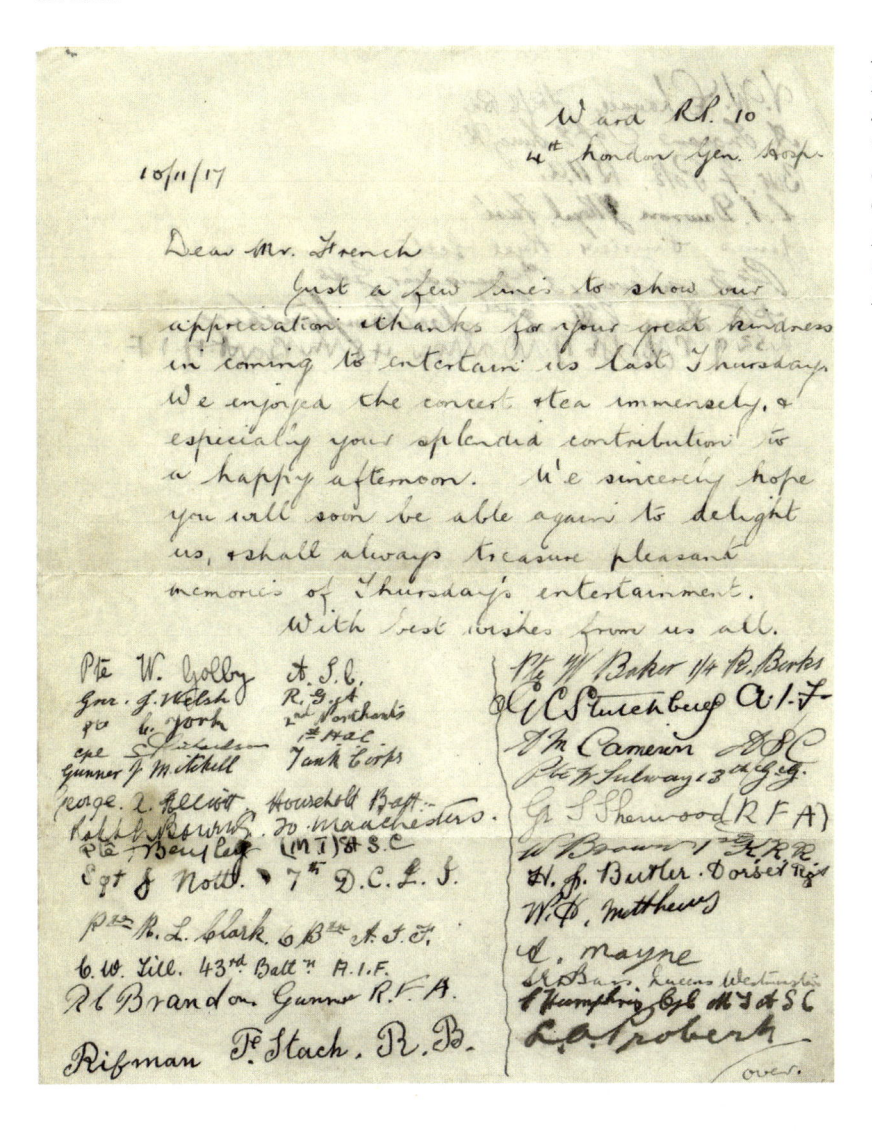

A letter from a London hospital signed by 25 wounded soldiers of different ranks and regiments.

Percy French Collection North Down Museum

Percy French sometimes travelled to France and Belgium on behalf of the Red Cross to entertain the wounded in hospitals. On at least one occasion he was accompanied by his then partner Betty Duncan. A poem called 'Meditations on Betty', written for the wedding of his talented and spirited former partner, includes the lines,

> *And when she sailed with me to France,*
> *The Captain never got a chance.*
> *She swept the sea with eagle glance*
> *And held the tiller.*

His watercolour 'The Ghost of Ypres' is stark evidence of his visits to Belgium and is a dramatic and poignant image of that much embattled and eventually ruined ancient city. It says more than words about the horror and futility of war. Most of the battles, like the Somme, were confined to a single year but at Ypres there were four or five major battles over a period of four years. It was what, according to a recent comment by Irish Times journalist Ronan McGreevy, caused Winston Churchill to say, 'I should like to acquire the whole of the ruins of Ypres … a more sacred place for the British race does not exist in the world.'

'The Ghost of Ypres'

Watercolour by Percy French

Percy French Collection North Down Museum

29. 'WHEN THE STORY'S NEARLY ENDED'

From the poem 'Later On' by Percy French

Mrs De Burgh Daly's husband, a renowned medical doctor living in Dublin at the time, managed to get Percy French to bed for a week during the flu epidemic of 1918. French insisted on sitting up and painting sketches from memory. During that summer French and May Laffan rehearsed at De Burgh Daly's house, 'often filling the garden with melody'. Ominously, she also mentions that even on the warmest days, her brother tended to feel cold and chilly.

Everything suggests that May Laffan was a vital support to French in his final years. His youngest daughter Joan remembered 'a solo banjoist, charming person and full of fun'. Old playbills mention their 'New Recital' being performed in Bundoran and at Dublin's Lyric and Molesworth Halls. His haunting song, 'Innismeela', a lament for lost love, was, according to James N. Healy in his *Songs of Percy French*, known to be sung by French's young partner. But it was not all happening in Ireland or in partnership with May Laffan. A *Daily Telegraph* review of *Humours of Art and Music* – performed at the Steinway Hall for a week in January 1919, with Sterndale Bennett replacing Dr Collisson as French's partner – reveals French's determination to maintain his reputation at a city location with which he was so long associated.

He and Lennie celebrated their silver wedding on 24 January, when in his usual light-hearted fashion, he committed his feelings to verse:

> *If we had lived upon our lone and never married – golly*
> *By now an ancient cat I'd own and you a pretty polly,*
> *But such a course I think we've shown*
> *Had been surprising folly*
> *For where would Ettie be! and Joan!*
> *And need I mention Mollie!*

Advertisement for a London show with May La Fan

Percy French Collection North Down Museum

Ettie has acknowledged that towards the end of 1919 her father collapsed at an engagement in Surrey and immediate engagements were cancelled. Although 'very frail' and despite entreaties from family and friends, French was unwilling to give up his touring schedule. He really enjoyed touring 'especially with his cheery, gay collaborator, Miss May Laffan'. On 6 January 1920 French's great friend Collisson wrote to him from the Swiss winter sports resort of Wengen (where Collisson was raising funds for his 'Waifs and Strays' charity and where he had sold some paintings for French): 'How we wish you were with us! Every night, *nem con*, the audience sends you a message hoping you will soon be well again.' This letter suggests that Percy French was not well enough to undertake the trip to Switzerland and hardly strong enough to honour an engagement for himself and 'Miss May La Fan' at Glasgow's Palette Club on the evening of 16 January 1920. This staging of 'Song, Story, Chalk and Banjo Solos' was fated to be his final performance.

Although unwell on the morning of the performance, French insisted on fulfilling his commitment at a Club where he always received a special welcome. May Laffan anxiously saw him off for Liverpool the following day where, at his cousin Canon Richardson's home in Formby, he intended to rest. Percy French thanked her for the way she had 'played the game to the end'. Upon arriving home in Dublin she was upset and told her mother she had lost her best friend.

At Formby, the doctor pronounced that French had pneumonia. His wife Lennie came. Despite receiving the best professional nursing care, he died 'suddenly and painlessly' after an illness of four days, but not before he penned some final lines in honour of his aunt Mary Anne, Canon Richardson's ninety-seven-year-old mother:

> *Aunt Mary Anne, Aunt Mary Anne,*
> *The sole Survivor of the Clan,*
> *Who laughed, and danced, and romped, and ran*
> *In dear old Clooniquin!*
> *I write these lines when in my bed,*
> *Whereon I lay my weary head.*
> *Exhausted, sick, but not quite dead,*
> *And hardly worth a pin.*

'When the Story's Nearly Ended' 145

In a letter to Percy French's wife Lennie, Dr Houston Collisson ('The Little Doctor', as French often called him) referred to French's love for Newman's hymn, 'Lead, Kindly Light' and particularly the lines, 'O'er moor and fen, o'er crag and torrent / Till the night is gone'. These lines are engraved on the base of the cross marking French's grave in the lovely churchyard of St Luke's parish in Formby. Dr Collisson himself died suddenly, just a day after conducting a memorial service for his great friend.

French's grave in St Luke's Churchyard, Formby, Merseyside
Percy French Society Archive

French painting the 'Haycocks at Cloonyquin'
Percy French Collection North Down Museum

'Haycocks at Cloonyquin'
Watercolour by Percy French
Percy French Collection North Down Museum

EPILOGUE

To reflect as meaningfully as possible on the life and times of Percy French it has been essential to use some extracts from his writings and from other creative works, works that were extraordinarily varied and prolific. Perhaps just one quarter of his output has been touched upon in this appraisal of a life of wonderful versatility. Doing it more complete justice would require in-depth analyses of all of his songs, poems, plays, recitations, parodies, and watercolours – an almost impossible task. As a practitioner of parody, an art that was re-emerging to an extent in the twentieth century, French is highly regarded by a number of critics. Unfortunately, we can never now experience his greatest gift of all: being able to engage across the footlights with audiences in the halls and platforms of almost every town in Ireland as well as the theatres, colleges and homes (including the Royal household) of Great Britain and a number of clubs and theatres in the major cities of North America.

One thing that perhaps we can agree on after our literary meanderings is that William Percy French was a person of independent and critical mind. All evidence implies that he did not accept the existing norms of the society or of the class in which he grew up. Reserved and ever an observer rather than a participator, one suspects that he envied the uninhibited gaiety so joyously reflected in 'Phil the Fluter's Ball.'

The entry for Percy French in the publication *Who's Who, 1909* gives a succinct summary of his background and his main accomplishments at that time. We know not the extent of his personal input in this prestigious volume but it is somewhat amusing and typically 'Percy French' to find 'Phil the Fluter's Ball' mentioned next to French's 'having painted some Irish scenes for the King'. His recreations are given as 'cycling, lawn tennis, water-colour sketching and writing pathetic poems'.

'Writing pathetic poems' is at first sight a rather enigmatic phrase. It leaves us wondering whether French, in characteristic tongue-in-cheek manner, was trying to avoid the pretention that might be associated with this high-sounding publication. It might also be a reference to a limited number of poems that are sometimes regarded as inspired by the death of his first wife. 'Gortnamona', for instance, is beautiful but deeply sad and with an obvious element of pathos. It was later sensitively put to music by Philip Green for Brendan O'Dowda:

> *Long, long ago, in the woods of Gortnamona,*
> *I thought the wind was sighing round the blackthorn tree,*
> *But oh! it was the banshee that was crying, crying, crying,*
> *And I knew my love was dying far across the sea.*

However, it can also be contended that there is a touch of pathos in most of Percy French's songs and poems, even in those that are regarded as his 'comic songs'. After all, there are losers in songs like 'Donnegan's Daughter' and 'McBreen's Heifer'! Maybe the word 'pathetic' in the *Who's Who, 1909* entry is used to mean inadequate, feeble or woeful, in an attempt to play down any suggestion of self-defined poetic worthiness.

French's lifetime love of the game of lawn tennis is reflected in the poem 'Tennis':

> *In the world's great game of tennis*
> *Which from pole to pole is seen*
> *Let love be the point of starting,*
> *Faults be few and far between;*
> *Raise no unseemly racket,*
> *From base lines of life break loose,*
> *Win no underhand advantage;*
> *This moral we deduce.*

It is a simple but clever example of the kind of amusing metaphorical wordplay that French was prone to practise. It may also, in a slightly deeper sense, express something of his personal philosophy of life. His sister mentions French lifetime 'enjoyment' of the game of tennis. His daughter Ettie writes of her father patiently teaching her and her sisters how to play and also of going with him to the 'old Wimbledon' where the underhand service was still practised and where American May Sutton was the first to wear her skirts up to her knees.

French's ability to communicate with children is evident both in anecdote and in a number of his works. His children's play *Noah's Ark*, with its cast of fairies and animals, was successfully staged at London's Waldorf Theatre. Letters written to his children were full of wordplay, jokey references and amusing drawings. According to Ettie, when at home French would join his daughters after lunch in a 'game of frogs', which meant leaping all round the table even though 'he was nearly fifty at the time'. His monologue 'The Children's Party', for so long an item in his platform recitals, evokes with philosophical humour the chaotic nature of such well-intentioned family activity. During the flourishing Edwardian years, drawing-room plays were staged at 27 Clifton Hill. These involved both his young family and special friends from the world of entertainment like Hill Rowan and Alice Linde. One such play, *The Rival Magicians*, was set in 'The Throne Room in the Palace of old Stoneybroke'! Lines from his poem 'Later On' remind us of his struggles to cope with both the financial and the parental demands of life even in his most successful years:

> *You'll learn that what's enough for one is not enough for two,*
> *Nor enough for half a dozen later on.*
> *No, the work is never ended though for holidays you crave,*
> *There are pop-guns to be mended for the Robbers in the Cave.*
> *You fancy you're the master, but you find that you're a slave*
> *To a curly headed tyrant later on.*

French's faults were surely few and far between. It was his carelessness in money matters that may be considered his major weakness. A 'disregard for his own and his family's prosperity', as his sister Mrs De Burgh Daly wrote, was one of his greatest faults. However, it should be said that it was most certainly not a case of spending money for his own comforts, about which he was both careless and frugal. Notwithstanding this apparent thoughtlessness in money matters, his daughter detected a sense of a materialistic responsibility in her father's ideas to invest in a house of his own and to give his children some specific professional training. These proposals were 'turned down by the family, who saw nothing but the rosy present in a peaceful world.' Sadly, as we know, World War I brought an end to such a philosophy.

French's all-consuming but disorganized approach to his professional life relied hugely on the support and patience of his wife Lennie. *The Jarvey* journal could only have survived its short existence with the assistance of true friends like Richard Orpen and Eddy Radcliffe. Much of the organization for his Irish tours required unselfish organizational support from people such as Mason, Franklin and Collisson. Although French suffered life's disappointments and frustrations stoically and humorously, his emotions very occasionally spilled over into more violent reactions, for example in the face of perceived unfairness or slight to his wife or another female.

R.J. Mecredy, writing in *The Irish Cyclist*, recounts that although French's equanimity was marvellous he did lose his composure at least once. Whilst French was singing on stage an individual commenced booing and hooting. French withstood the interruptions up to the third verse when he stopped short, stalked down the hall, grabbed the offender and, to borrow a euphemism from his song 'Come Back, Paddy Reilly', 'assisted him' down the outside steps. Then, with an unruffled front, he returned to the platform and continued with his song.

French's historical satires and short plays need to be interpreted by the best professionals. These include the already mentioned publication, *The First Lord Liftenant*, a travesty of the historical story of the relationship between Queen Elizabeth I and the Earl of Essex. The more contemporary recitation 'The Queen's After-dinner Speech' (as overheard and recited by the deputy-assistant-waiter at the Vice-Regal Lodge) purports to show Queen Victoria's awareness of the politics and social nuances in Ireland. It is written in what the critic Vivian Mercier described as a parody of an old Irish verse format, one with a long history in Anglo-Irish humorous writing. It starts:

> 'Me loving subjects, sez she,
> 'Here's me best respects', sez she.

It is not unlikely that some of the words French imagined Her Majesty uttering are somewhat suggestive of his own scepticism about the politically motivated leanings of W.B. Yeats and his muse, the English-born Irish nationalist Maud Gonne:

> *'An' I think there's a slate,' sez she,*
> *'Off Willie Yeats,' sez she,*
> *'He should be at home,' sez she,*
> *'French polishin' a pome,' sez she,*
> *'An' not writin' letters,' sez she,*
> *'About his betters,' sez she,*

And:

> *'That Maud Gonne,' sez she,*
> *'Dhressin' in black,' sez she,*
> *'To welcome me back,' sez she,*

It has been said that the nature of the poet is the pursuit of the ideals of truth and wisdom. Although French himself would likely see this as a rather lofty aspiration, it does seem that he always looked beyond immediate impressions. People and events were not taken at face value. He distrusted and undermined the grandiose, the sensational and the ostentatious with a gentle satirical humour. It is perhaps this facet of French's style that always brings a smile when his name is mentioned.

The irony and satire are of course balanced by an underlying tolerance and indeed respect for human nature in all its moods and contradictions. Although French's social style was mainly witty and urbane, he was also capable of expressing the deepest of human emotion (almost always in verse), as in the context of the death of his first wife.

Comparing French to James Joyce may well, at first sight, be considered incongruous. It is known that Joyce might have preferred a musical career as a singer and French on the other hand followed a more literary path. And they were both parodists, in the sense that they questioned the more accepted mores of society. Joyce's *Finnegans Wake* often include lines from Percy French, albeit in typically distorted form. In his introduction to the Penguin edition of Joyce's *Ulysses* Declan Kiberd notes that *Ulysses* is itself a parody of the classical story of the 'heroic' Odysseus with the central character (Bloom) as the common man rather than some mythical conquering figure. Joyce wished to scale grandiose claims down to a human dimension and to focus on the domestic rather than the epic. He also saw worship of the heroic ultimately leading to the glorification of violence and warfare. It is surely not too fanciful to view Percy French in a similar light.

Professor Kiberd also sees Joyce's work as 'reducing the vast claims made for art by the Romantics'. This reminds us of French's parodying of poets like Wordsworth, Browning and Tennyson; he rewrote well-known nursery rhymes in the more high-flown language of such worthy literary figures.

> Little Bo-Peep (rewritten by French in Wordsworth's style):
> *I walked with her upon the hill,*
> *Her grief was very deep,*
> *Her tears were running like a rill,*
> *For she had lost her sheep.*

In an early letter to Lennie, French wrote of spending time at the National Gallery in London trying to learn from J.M.W. Turner, the great romantic painter. Like French, Turner was initially inspired by 'ash in the sky' and is known for his images of the awe-inspiring power of nature and of landscapes dramatically transformed by the Industrial Revolution. In contrast to Turner's 'crimson flush' and his amazing skies, French's style is gentler and he paints the rural landscape that he loved. Like most artists of his time, French was motivated by the almost spiritual effect of light, whether he was capturing a scene from his experiences in Ireland, England, Switzerland or North America.

It is of course not particularly appropriate to compare Percy French the artist with artists like Turner, or to compare Percy French the writer with writers like Yeats, Wilde or Joyce. French's greatness lies in his incredible renaissance-style versatility and his witty and humorous sensitivity to the human condition. Voltaire's maxim, 'All the Arts are brothers, each one a light to the other', seems appropriate. It must be remembered however that 'all the arts' had of necessity taken second place to the main thrust of French's career as a professional entertainer.

In her memoir *Willie*, French's daughter Ettie explains that after his death, people's attempts to describe him often just ended with the simple statement, 'Ah, there never was anyone like him.' More specifically, she wrote. 'Willie was no politician and no highbrow; he took no part in any of the national or literary movements then afoot. In fact he dug gentle fun at them all without offending anyone too deeply.' French's feeling was always for the individual, he never identified with groups, literary sets or political factions.

He never became a fully paid member of London's famous Savage Club, which had held him in such high esteem. Though we may view these aspects of Percy French's character in a positive light they may however have been something of a hindrance to achieving wider literary acclaim. W.H. Auden has written that there are many writers whose works are better than their lives. We might conclude that, in the case of Percy French, they are one and the same thing.

An unusual but rather charming side-line of French's eclectic mixture of talents was the creation of albums of his poems, each illustrated by an appropriate watercolour on the facing page. These artefacts, scarce, unique to Percy French and by now highly collectable, were normally gifted to friends or created in memory of a special occasion. In one of them, the poem 'Here and Hereafter' is illustrated by his watercolour sketch of light cascading from beneath a darkish cloud to a sea of breaking waves:

Album of Irish sketches by Percy French

Percy French Society Archive

The wide wide sea
Is a joy to see
I stand by that heaving plain,
And feast mine eyes
On the sunset skies
And the distant mountain chain.
It makes one think
How the hills will shrink
And the ocean seem a pond,
When we stand by the sea
Of Eternity,
And wonder what lies beyond.

Percy French
Collection North
Down Museum

MEMORIAL FUND

After the death of Percy French his friends and admirers established a memorial fund. They believed that it was appropriate to assist his widow and three daughters, who had been left inadequately provided for. They felt that although he was a national asset 'he never had obtained anything like a fair pecuniary recompense for the work that he did.' Despite having given the public more than he received in return, French died a 'poor man.'

As was already mentioned, the talent for acquiring and keeping money formed no part of French's make-up. Nonetheless, it should be said that other factors apart from his acknowledged carelessness in business matters contributed to his lack of accumulated capital. French was aged over forty before he committed to a successful career as a professional entertainer and after a relatively short period this major source of his income was dealt 'a mortal blow' by the social changes brought about by the outbreak of war in 1914. He was also unconditionally generous, devoting time and talents to charitable causes. On his death the many newspaper obituaries were warmly appreciative of his inimitable entertainments, which had drawn audiences from all parts of the United Kingdom and had earned him a world-wide reputation.

The President of the Memorial Fund was Sir John Ross, French's friend from college days, and the executive committee contained other close friends and former colleagues such as L.H. Brindly, Katherine Tynan-Hinkson, R.C. Orpen and J.C. Percy. R.J. Mecredy, James Duncan and Major F.B. Craig acted as Hon. Secretaries.

IF

If I should die to-night.
And you should come,
And stand beside me,
Lying cold and dumb,
And if while standing there,
You whispered low,
'Here's the ten pounds
You lent me years ago.'
I would arise although they'd laid me flat,
And say, 'What's that?'

If I should die to-night,
But rose to count,
With trembling fingers,
That long lost amount,
I might live on; But when
You said, 'Here's your umbrella
And your fountain pen,'
For one short space
I'd gaze into thy face
And then – drop dead again.

Parody by Percy French of
'If I should die' by Benjamin
Franklin King, 1857-94

AS OTHERS REMEMBERED HIM

My father is remembered now chiefly as a songwriter, but oddly enough song writing was just one of his side-lines. He was what was then called a society entertainer and that meant a lot of travelling and sometimes long absences on tour ... I like, as he did, to be on the move, and in his case dislike of standing still and doing nothing went as far as jumping impatiently on the wrong bus if the right one failed to appear.

Ettie French

He had Sir Harry Lauder's extraordinary power of 'stepping over the footlights,' and chatting familiarly with his audience as though at a family party – which really is the entertainer's highest art.

Hill Rowan

A small boy, nine or ten years old, sitting in a draughty Concert Hall on the strand at Skerries, enthralled by stories and songs and magical drawings, all done with effortless ease by an uncle-ish sort of man who had the gift of charming both young and old, and holding them for two whole hours alone and unaided – that's my earliest memory of Percy French. It must have been about 1902 ... At Thomond House, Lisdoonvarna, I saw him do one of those clever pictures on a china plate – with naught but candle-smoke and a match stick. It was a miracle to see the picture grow.

Colm O'Lochlainn
July 1984

I know of no man who brought more wholesome entertainment and genuine laughter to his generation and such was the quality of his great gifts that his best works still hold a charm for any worthwhile human being in this present age of values so very different from those which he recognized.

Richard Hayward

His sense of character, keen observation and genial satire on the foibles of human nature, together with his remarkable skill with his pencil, combine to make him an ideal entertainer.

The Referee
14 January 1912

I remember W.P.F. there [Bundoran] with May Laffan. My mother invited him to tea. He asked 'Have you any sugar?' and the answer being in the affirmative, he said 'I'll come' ... [my friend] Peggy said 'Oh Mr French yesterday evening was the happiest in my life [his concert in the hall near the Railway Station].' 'That's the sort of criticism I like; you are on the free list for tonight.'

Molly Greeves
6 September 2006

His first name being William, he was always known to us children as Uncle Willie, and was our favourite uncle. Looking back now on the years, my memories of his visits to us were of music and painting. Directly he arrived, out would come the banjo – later the guitar – and he would sing away while we joined with gusto in the choruses. A table would then be cleared, and we would gather round, while out came his paintbox and brushes, water and a painting block. Giving us each a sheet of this and a paint brush, he would start at the top, painting in the blue sky.

Maeve Kenny
quoted in A Picture of Percy French by Alan Tongue

Discerning art lovers and connoisseurs have not failed to appreciate the subtle mastery of perspective and colour that is the chief characteristic of his style nor, the exquisite ease with which he can express the effects of light and shade.

Oliver Nulty
Lead Kindly Light – Celebrating 150 Years of Percy French

THE PERCY FRENCH COLLECTION

Digest of the collection of watercolour paintings and memorabilia in the trusteeship of the Percy French Society and administered by North Down Museum, Bangor, Co. Down

Watercolours

The collection includes some ninety watercolours by Percy French. Most were bequeathed to the Society trustees by French's daughters and other relatives. A number were donated by generous friends of the Society and some were purchased by the Society from its own resources.

French painted prolifically throughout most of his adult life, usually and ideally to express the talent that he enjoyed most of all. Sometimes his work was generously presented to friends or given in return for hospitality received.

Perhaps the genre or subject matter most often identified as a 'Percy French' is the partly romantic and partly melancholic depiction of light breaking through rainy skies over moorland and distant mountain. He painted these profusely during his London years to augment his income as an entertainer and to meet a special demand for landscape painting, an idyllic antidote to the city and industrial scene.

The collection includes many paintings originally owned by his family and provides an insight to a wider choice of subject. It captures his experiences on his travels to Canada, USA and West Indies when at the height of his career as an entertainer.

In 1998 a substantial grant from the Heritage Lottery Fund provided 90 per cent of the cost of professional restoration of the watercolours, a project undertaken by the Percy French Society for the watercolours' preservation in the longer term. The paintings and other items were subsequently placed in the care and management of the North Down Museum so that they might be accessible for public research and exhibition.

Memorabilia

Box No.1 *Catalogue F01/ 01 - 32 etc.*
*Photographs pre -1900

Includes early family, Cavan days, the comic opera *The Knight of the Road*, second wife, Lennie, and children, Ettie and Mollie.

Box No.2 *Catalogue F02/01 - 68 + x02/69*
*Photographs post -1900

Includes daughters Ettie, Mollie and Joan, French the professional entertainer, life in London, Dr Houston Collisson, French with banjo, Paddy Reilly, Cloonyquin.

Box No.3 *Catalogue F03/01 - 109*
*Programmes and Reviews

Includes French's Cavan and Dublin years (1883-1900), the comic opera *The Knight of the Road*, French's professional career as an entertainer in Ireland, London, Manchester etc, final show in Glasgow 1920.

Press reviews from *The Irish Times, The Tatler, The Scotsman, The Daily Telegraph, The Times,* etc.

Box No.4 *Catalogue F04/01 - 65*
*Letters

French to wife, Lennie (F04/65 itself includes 62 letters written by French to Lennie before marriage in 1894). Also French's letters to his children and to his friend, R.J.Mecredy.

Letter from Sandringham to French on behalf of Princess of Wales (thanking him for leaving a smoke plate and book of watercolours). Letters from Lord Wolseley, Dr W.H. Collisson, etc.

Box No.5 *Catalogue FO5/03-13*
* **French's Professional Engagement Diaries 1900-1920**

These diaries, kept by his wife Lennie, also include family engagements.

Box No.6 *Catalogue FO6/01- 67*
* **Various Pieces of French's Writings and Jottings**

Including poems 'Gortnamona' and 'To the West', also a booklet 'The Monologue Series' which includes 'Our Housewarming' and the satirical monologues 'The Queen's Advice to Lord Zetland before starting for Ireland' and 'The Queen's after-dinner speech on the occasion of her last visit to Ireland (as overheard and reported by Larry Flynn, waiter)'. Other important writings are the following: *Rackety Rhymes* (magazine), *The Fall of Fitz-illium* (magazine), *The First Lord Liftenant* [sic] (booklet), *The Foolish Little Frog* (children's book) and a writing entitled 'The Shanachie Tells a Story'.

A copy of *John Bull* dated 25 June 1902, with a contribution by French, is also included.

There are also many additional, incomplete or partially written items, pages from the 'The Trombone of Truth' and some fragments.

Box No.7 *Catalogue FO7/01 - 07*
*****Plays**

Printed libretto of *The Knight of the Road* 1891

Printed libretto of *The Irish Girl* (re-write of *The Knight of the Road*)

Typescript of *Noah's Ark* 1906

Typescript of *The Rival Magicians*'1907

Typescript of *The Banshee*

Printed vocal score *Freda and the Fairies* 1909

Box No. 8 *Catalogue F08/01-09*
*Plays Continued

Includes typescripts of 'King of the Mountains', 'La Belle Souris' (list of characters) and 'Gloom' (parody on Russian drama).

Box No. 9 *Catalogue FO9/01-23*
*Magazines (mostly parodies)

The Lawn Tennis Tournament, Buxton 1884

White Lines, Buxton 1885

Tennis Tournament, supplement to *The Irish Cyclist and Athlete*

Fitzwilliam Square – a Lawn Tennis Lay

Box No. 10 *Catalogue F10/01-73 and x10/76-89*
*Miscellaneous

Relating to Foyle College, Cavan, Savage Club (London), Glenveagh (Co. Donegal), *Who's Who, 1909, 1912,* Silver Wedding 1919, etc. French's B.A. Certificate, French's character told from his hand. Various press reports and photographs. Letter from Sir Hugh Lane to Mrs. French (undated). Drawings (sketches) 'The Divil a Thrain' and 'A Lion Story'. Passport application, letters received by his wife on French's death. Obituaries.

Box No. 11 *Catalogue F11/01-46 and x11/37-49*
*French the Artist

Includes press cuttings, photographs, sketches, drawings, together with pictures and verses about animals, also information re smoke pictures, catalogue for exhibition at New Dudley Galleries, London 1909, a review of an exhibition held at Modern Gallery, London and lists of paintings shown in various exhibitions.

Box No. 12 *Catalogue F12/01- 09*
*French's Cavan Years (1883-88)

Includes press cuttings from *Cavan Weekly News*, a copy of the home-produced magazine 'The Trombone of Truth', some photographs and the letter dismissing him as Inspector of Loans to Tenants dated July 1888.

Box No. 13 *Catalogue F13/01-56*
*****The Jarvey* (comic weekly edited by French 1888-90)**

Original issue dated 21 June, 1890. Photocopy of vol.1, no.1 of *The Jarvey* dated 3 January 1889. Sundry pages and transcripts from various issues of the weekly magazine, letters to/from contributors (particularly L. Brindley) and some pages from the *Irish Cyclist and Athlete*.

Box No. 14 *Catalogue F14/01-37*
*****American tour by French and Collisson**

Letters from French to family in London. Reviews by Canadian and USA newspapers. Poem 'Off to the West Indies' and various drawings, verses and posters. (See also his watercolour paintings.)

Box No. 15 *Catalogue F15/01-13*
*****Swiss tour**

Letters from French to his wife Lennie from Boulogne and from Swiss resorts such as St. Moritz, Grindewald, Engelberg and Adelboden (some with small drawings).

Box No. 16 *Catalogue F16/01-07*
*****Calendars and Cards**

Mostly postcards advertising some of French's songs, 'Phil the Fluter's Ball', 'Are Ye Right There, Michael?' and 'Slattery's Mounted Fut'. This box also includes the Christmas card printed in Canada for UNICEF (reproduction of a Swiss scene of winter sports by permission of the Oriel Gallery, Dublin).

Box No. 17 *Catalogue F17/01*
*****Unsorted press cuttings**

Box No. 18 *Catalogue F18/01-19*
*****Programmes and reviews re the stage show *The Golden Years***

Box No. 19 *Catalogue F19/01-19*
*****Scripts post 1920 (radio, television etc.)**

'With a Banjo on His Bike', 'Percy', 'Percy French Remembered', 'The Blarney Boys', 'Sweet Are My Dreams'.

Boxes No. 22 and 22A *Catalogue F22/01-01*
*SONGS, WORDS and MUSIC

(music by French unless stated otherwise – sometimes his friend and collaborator, Dr Collisson composed or arranged the music for French's later songs).

Abdul the Bulbul Ameer (pirated edition, French's words altered)

Ach I Dunno (music by Mollie French)

All by the Baltic Say (music by L. Braid)

Am Tag (music by French and L. Braid)

Andy McElroe (written and composed by French and John Ross)

Are Ye Right There, Michael? (music by Collisson, by French in later editions)

Bad Ballads for Badish Babes (music by Collisson)

Ballymilligan (music arranged by Alec Rowley)

Come Back, Paddy Reilly (music from a traditional air)

Cornelius Burke

The Darlin' Girl from Clare

Donnegan's Daughter (music by Collisson)

Drumcolliher

Eileen Oge (music traditional, arranged by Collisson)

The Emigrant Ship

The Fairies' Lough (Innismeela) (music by M. Bent)

Father O'Callaghan (music by Collisson)

Flanagan's Flying Machine (music by Collisson)

The Fortunes of Finnegan (music by Collisson)

Gortnamona (music by Philip Green)

Have We Not Airs and Graces (music by Collisson)

The Hoodoo (music by Collisson)

Innismeela

In the Studio (music by Isobel Crowe)

The Islands of Aran (music by Isobel Crowe)

Jim Whelahan's Automobile (music arranged by Collisson)

A Kerry Courting (music by Collisson)

The Killyran Wrackers (modern manuscript by Courtney Kenny)

King Edward in Erin (music by Collisson)

Kitty Gallagher

The Laird of Lantyloo (modern manuscript by Courtney Kenny)

Larry Mick McGarry

Little Bridget Flynn (traditional air arranged by Mollie French)

Luke the Looney (modern manuscript by Courtney Kenny)

McBreen's Heifer

Maguire's Motor Bike (music by Collisson)

A Man by the Name of Maguire

Mat Hannigan's Aunt

Mick's Hotel

The Mountains o' Mourne (music arranged by Collisson)

Mrs. Brady (music by Collisson)

Mulligan's Masquerade

Nell Flaherty's Drake

The Night that Miss Cooney Eloped

No More O'yer Golfin' For Me (music by Collisson)

The Oklahoma Rose

On the Road to Ballybay (music by Mollie French)

The Palace of Puck (words by French and T.H. Read, music by J.A. Robertson)

Phil the Fluter's Ball

Phishlin Phil McHugh

Pretendy Land (music by J.A. Robertson)

Rafferty's Racing Mare (music by Collisson)

Sing Me No Song (manuscript copy, music by Ettie French)

Slattery's Mounted Fut

Soldiers Three

The Snakes He Left Behind (photocopy from *The Jarvey*)

The Song of the UPS (music arranged by Ettie French)

That's That (music by Captain Mostyn)

That's Why We're Burying Him (music by Ettie French)

Three Blind Mice from 'Butterflies' (words by French and T.H. Read, music by J.A. Robertson)

Tullinahaw (music an Irish air, arranged by Collisson)

Wait for a While Now, Mary (music by Collisson)

When Erin Awakes (music by Collisson)

ACKNOWLEDGMENTS

This book, written on behalf of the Percy French Society, was an idea that emerged under the 2010-15 chairmanship of Dr David Capper. The idea was nobly and enthusiastically undertaken as a project by Ronnie Maxwell who deserves at least as much credit for the outcomes as the author. Ronnie was assisted by his team of 'co-editors': Edna Maxwell, Catherine Wright and Gladys O'Neill. I cannot overstate my appreciation of their confidence in me and of their patience and unfaltering support in bringing the project to fruition.

Likewise, the attractive style of the final product with its many illustrations owes much to the skill, imagination and enthusiasm of the design team; Michael O'Neill and Jonny Kane exhibited immense patience with the rather erratic approach of the author.

The North Down Museum, Bangor, Co. Down cares for The Percy French Collection, – some one hundred watercolours and approximately eight hundred items of memorabilia – which was entrusted to the Percy French Society by the family and relatives of Percy French as well as by many friends and supporters of the Society. My sincere appreciation is extended to the Museum's manager, Heather McGuicken, and particularly to her museum assistant, Leanne Briggs, for responding to my many requests for access to the Collection and for the technical support provided throughout. I trust that this book will also be an acknowledgement of the Percy French Society's valued relationship with the Museum.

The National Gallery of Ireland provided photographic images of paintings with much goodwill through the persons of Donal Maguire and Sinéad Farrelly. At the Hibernian Academy, Fernando Sanchez was equally helpful in providing information from the Academy's records. Teresa Connaghan at Glenveagh Castle in Donegal kindly provided important extracts from the Castle's old visitors' book. The Chairman of Fitzwilliam Lawn Tennis Club, Frank Egan, and the Club's Financial Controller, Eoghan Williams, responded most generously to my request for material from their archives.

Acknowledgments

I must also acknowledge the ever-kindly cooperation of the County Roscommon Percy French Society in the persons of its chairperson, Father Francis Beirne, committee member Tom Lynch and Richie Farrell, Chief Librarian for the county. I am grateful to the directors of the National Famine Museum at Strokestown Park, Co. Roscommon for the use of a photographic image of the house and grounds. Cavan County Museum in Ballyjamesduff, specifically Margaret Mortimer, responded to my requests for photographs with the utmost alacrity. I am also pleased to acknowledge the helpfulness of Mr Liam Henry, Hon. Secretary of Co. Cavan Golf Club, in providing information about Lord Farnham (family name Maxwell) and the Farnham estate.

Michael Slevin of the Engineering School at Trinity College, Dublin readily updated me on the 'Museum Building' where William Percy French studied and where one of French's watercolours hangs.

Declan Kiberd, Professor of Irish Studies at the University of Notre Dame, graciously allowed me to quote from his works. Charles U. Daly, Director Emeritus of the John F. Kennedy Library Foundation, was likewise happy to be quoted in my writings.

My friends Max Corbett and Gray Horner were ever willing to give some technical know-how in the provision of images for the book. Paul Clements kindly gave me a copy of Richard Hayward's article in the *Belfast Telegraph* of 23 January 1960. Courtney Kenny readily allowed me to include the watercolour sketch of Cloonyquin House, where William Percy French was born. Alan Tongue's intimate knowledge of Percy French and his family was often useful to me in clarifying some finer points.

Brian M. Walker, the Emeritus Professor of Irish Studies at Queen's University Belfast, provided valuable advice with regard to design and publishing for which I am grateful.

Finally, I wish to acknowledge the vision of the founder of the Percy French Society, Oscar Rollins. Oscar's deeply felt regard for Percy French, which was manifested in an unyielding determination that French should not be forgotten, was inspirational in my developing an interest that is marked by this publication.

BIBLIOGRAPHY

Butler, Patricia. *Three Hundred Years of Irish Watercolours and Drawings* (Weidenfeld and Nicholson: London 1990)

Collisson, W.A. Houston. *Dr Collisson In and On Ireland* (Robert Sutton: London 1908)

Daly, Mrs De Burgh, ed. *Chronicles and Poems of Percy French* (Talbot Press: Dublin 1922)

Daly, Mrs De Burgh, ed. *Prose, Poems and Parodies of Percy French* (Talbot Press Ltd: Dublin 1925)

Ferris, Tom. *Irish Railways: A New History* (Gill and Macmillan: Dublin 2008)

French, Ettie. *Willie* (The Percy French Society: North Down, 1994)

French, Percy, ed. *The Jarvey* (Mecredy and Kyle: Dublin 1889-90)

Healy, James N. *The Songs of Percy French* (Mercier Press: Cork 1983)

Healy, James N. *Percy French and his Songs* (Mercier Press: Cork 1966)

McDowell, Jim. *Beyond the Lights* (Nonsuch Publishing: Dublin 2007)

Montgomery, Bob. *R.J. Mecredy: The Father of Irish Motoring* (Dreoilin Publications: Dublin 2003)

Moran, Gerard and Raymond Gillespie, eds. *Galway History and Society* (Geography Publications: Dublin 1996)

Nulty, Oliver. *Lead Kindly Light* (The Oriel Gallery: Dublin 2004)

O'Connor, Ulick. *The Fitzwilliam Story* (Richview Brown & Nolan: Dublin 1977)

O'Dowda, Brendan. *The World of Percy French* (Blackstaff Press: Belfast 1981)

Ross, John. *The Years of my Pilgrimage* (Edward Arnold: London 1924)

Tongue, Alan. *A Picture of Percy French* (Greystone Books: Antrim 1990)

Tongue, Alan, *The Love Letters of Percy French and more besides* (The Lilliput Press: Dublin 2016)

INDEX OF PERSONS AND PLACES

Alberti, Margarita, 20, 21, 23
Alexandra, Queen, 112
Anglesey, 112
Annesley, Lord, 60
Aoife, 15
Armagh, 128
Armytage Moore, Ethel (see also French, Mrs E.K.), 10, 57, 58, 64, 67, 72, 89, 90
Armytage Moore, Hugh, 57
Athlone, 86
Auden, W.H., 152
Avoca, 72, 81

Backhouse, Marmaduke, 39
Baldoyle, 83
Ballinasloe, 128
Ballinrobe, 128
Ballybay, 2, 58, 59, 66
Ballycastle, 106
Ballyconnell, 86
Ballybunion, 130, 131
Ballyjamesduff, 125, 126, 169
Ballymoney, 128
Ballyporeen, 107
Bangor (County Down), 62, 106, 128, 159, 168
Barton, Mrs, 33
Baxter, Stanley, 62
Beaumont, Henry, 79
Belgium, 142
Belfast, 62, 66, 75, 78, 83, 114, 129, 132, 169
Bennett, Sterndale, 143
Bermuda, 117, 122

Birmingham, George, 63
Blackrock, 139, 140
Boston, 63, 121, 135
Boylan, Patricia, 138
Bradford, 102, 139
Brighton, 102, 139
Brindley, 153
Bristol, 21
Brittany, 103
Broadstone, 96
Brooke, Colonel & Mrs, 72, 81
Browning, 151
Bundoran, 31, 54, 106, 132, 143, 158
Burke, Patricia, 140
Burke, Sarah, 19, 23
Burke, Ulick, 19
Burmington, 87, 90
Burns, 10
Butler, Mildred Anne, 114
Buxton, 55, 60, 62

Caesar, Julius, 63
Cambridge, 116
Canada, 46, 117, 159
Cardiff, 74, 102
Carlow, 128
Carrickfergus, 17, 19
Castleknock, 103
Cavan, 45-61, 64, 66, 114, 125, 126, 128, 160
Chaucer, 73
Christie, Gerald, 95
Churchill, Winston, 142
Claregalway, 19

Clifden, 106
Cloonyquin, 10, 18-30, 32, 34, 35, 76, 81, 102, 145, 160, 169
Cohen, Sheldon S., 20
Cole, Mrs, 49, 56
Coleraine, 66, 128
Collie, Derek, 63
Collisson, Dr Houston, 12, 74, 78, 79, 84, 85, 88, 91, 92, 93, 97, 99, 100, 107, 108, 117, 118, 120, 123, 124, 134, 136, 140, 143, 144, 145, 149, 160
Connemara, 106, 131
Conradi, Peter J., 9
Cookstown, 128
Cootehill, 125
Cork, 63, 66, 78, 128
Cornwall, 92
Corofin, 97
Craig, Major F.B., 155
Croke Park, 126
Cromwell, Oliver, 18, 71, 162
Crumit, Frank, 43, 44

Daly, Charles U., 63, 169
Daly, Kevin, 43
Davis, Judith, 19, 23
Davos, 135
De Burgh Daly, Mrs, 10, 13, 15, 24, 25, 26, 28, 30, 32, 40, 45, 57, 81, 116, 118, 139, 140, 143, 148
De Burgo, Sir Richard, 18
De Nash, Seamus, 25
Denny, Ernest, 105
Devon, 88, 113
Donaghadee, 14
Donegal, 27, 109, 118
Doyle, Conan, 72

D'Oyly Carte, 88
Drominchin, 61
Drumcolliher, 53, 91
Dubedat, Miss, 79
Dublin, 17, 22, 34, 35, 36, 41, 42, 54, 57, 60, 66, 69, 71, 72, 74, 78, 79, 81-90, 93, 96, 101-05, 114, 124, 126, 128, 137- 44
Duff, J.C., 117
Dumfries, 102
Duncan, Betty, 137-9, 142
Duncan, Ellie, 138
Duncan, Jim, 138, 155
Dundrum (Co. Down), 17
Dungannon, 66, 128
Dunlavin, 95
Du Val, 86

Eastbourne, 139
Edenderry, 128
Edward, King, 101, 107, 108, 112
Eisenhower, Dwight D., 44
Eliot, George, 63
Elizabeth I, Queen, 71, 149
Elphin, 10, 25
Engelberg, 134
England, 44, 55, 71, 78, 91, 92, 95, 100, 102, 128, 151
Ennis, 96, 128
Essex, Lord, 71

Farnham, Lord, 53, 57
Fernandez, Juan, 122
Ferris, Tom, 129
Finea, Bridge of, 125
Folkstone, 102
Formby, 13, 38, 102, 144, 145
Foster, Stephen, 36

Index of Persons and Places

Foyle College, 34, 45, 54
France, 18, 128, 142
Franklin, Mr H., 127, 130, 131, 149
Freeney, Jack, 79
French, Arthur (died 1712), 18, 23, 102
French, Arthur (died 1729), 19, 23
French, Arthur (died 1789), 19, 20, 23
French, Arthur John St George, 23
French, Christopher (died 1797), 20, 76
French, Christopher (died 1897), 23, 24, 26
French, Ettie (daughter), 10, 13, 20, 22, 26, 29, 50, 51, 57, 81, 82, 83, 90, 98, 113, 115, 124, 139, 143, 144, 147, 148, 152, 157
French, Henry Walter, 20
French, Joan, 13, 90, 122, 123
French, John, 20, 21, 23
French, Maeve Pauline Alberti, 21
French, Mollie, 67, 68, 72, 74, 80, 90
French, Mrs E.K., 67, 68, 72, 80, 82
French, Susan, 24
French, Percy, *passim*
Fuller, Loie, 88
Furniss, Harry, 86

Gaiety Theatre, 36, 62
Galileo, 39
Galway, 7, 18, 23, 102
Gibbs, Captain Brandreth, 134
Gilbert & Sullivan, 84
Glasgow, 102, 144
Glaslough, 127

Glendalough, 53
Glenveagh Castle, 109
Godley, A.D., 46, 88, 90
Godley, Rev. James, 61
Gonne, Maud, 150
Gortnamona, 147
Green, Philip, 147
Greeves, Mollie, 158
Grossmith, George, 86
Guildo, Brittany, 104

Hamilton, 91
Hammond, J.W., 74, 76
Hampshire, 113
Hanley, Mrs, 83
Hannay, Canon, 63
Harding, 53
Harkness, W., 57
Harris, Dorothea Helen, 22
Harwich, 102
Hastings, Ernest, 118
Hayes, Claude, 114
Hayward, Richard, 157, 169
Healy, James N., 13, 42, 141, 143
Higgins, Michael D., 108
Higgins, Tom, 54
Holloway, Stanley, 140
Howth, 102, 106

Irwin, Sir Alfred, 20, 23

Jamaica, 122
Johnson, J. St A., 34, 109
Joyce, James, 14, 150
Jungfrau, 116, 136

Kaiser, Wilhelm, 27, 91
Kaye, Danny, 140

Kennedy, Mary, 50
Kenny, Courtney, 7, 25, 169
Kenny, Maeve, 158
Kerry, 109, 131, 140
Kiberd, Declan, 150, 151, 169
Kilcoole, 94
Kilkee, 96, 97, 102
Kilkenny, 17, 19, 86
Killarney, 52
King, Benjamin Franklin, 156
Kingston, 120, 121
Kipling, Rudyard, 104
Kirk Langley, 32, 33
Kirwin, Mary, 19
Klosters, 135
Krakotoa, 56

Laffan, May, 137, 143, 144, 158
Lahinch, 97
Lartigue, Charles, 130
Las Vegas, 130
Lawford, H.F., 70, 71
Leeds, 102, 113
Le Fanu, Mr, 48
Leitrim, County, 7, 22, 61
Lever, Charles, 94
Limavady, 128
Limerick, 128
Linde, Alice, 87, 91, 148
Listowel, 130
Liverpool, 113, 144
Lloyd, Kitty, 138
London, 12, 62, 84, 88, 91, 106,
    112, 113, 114, 117, 118, 126, 128,
    131, 139, 140, 141, 144 148
Londonderry, Marchioness of, 112
Longfellow, Henry Wadsworth, 51
Loughrea, 127

Lucerne, 134
Ludlow, Miss Bessie, 36
Lusaka, 62
Lynmouth, 88

Macaulay, Lord, 70
MacGill, Patrick, 27
MacLise, Daniel, 16
Maeve, Queen, 21
Mahon, Denis, 29
Malahide, 106
Manners, Charles, 45
Marks, Florence, 137
Martin, Mr, 93
Mason, 149
Maude, Caroline, 109
May, Phil, 118
Mayne, Lt. Col. 'Paddy' Blair, 91
Mayo, 18, 131, 133
McCarthy, Jakes, 66
McCormack, John Count, 91
McDowell, Jim, 95
McGreevy, Ronan, 142
McGuinness, Bingham, 114
Mease, Dr & Mrs, 53
Mecredy, R.J., 52, 53, 64, 65, 66,
    71, 72, 149, 155
Mercier, Vivian, 149
Milne, 38
Miltown Malbay, 96
Minorca, 20
Monks Eleigh, 7
Montgomery, Bob, 71
Montreal, 120
Morton, Charles, 95
Moscow, 130
Motherwell, 102
Mount Jerome, 81, 82

Index of Persons and Places

Mulholland, Patricia, 62
Mullingar, 128
Myles na gCopaleen, 63

Naas, 128
Napoleon, 63
Newcastle, 106, 129
Newry, 128
Newtownstewart, 131
New York, 162
Niagara, 122
North, Thomas, Maj. General U. S. Army (Ret.), 44
Nottingham, 102

O'Brien, Father P.J., 62
O'Dowda, Brendan, 7, 13, 43, 44, 62, 107, 116, 139, 147
Oldcastle, 66, 125
O'Lochlainn, Colm, 157
Orpen, Richard, C., 64, 65, 66, 69, 71, 80, 85, 86, 88, 89, 91, 114, 149, 155
Osman Pasca, 42
Owen, Wilfred, 27
Oxford University, 24, 46, 89, 116

Paddington, 118
Panama, 117, 123
Parnell, Charles Stewart, 32, 33
Percy, J.C., 155

Percy, Susan Emma, 23
Pigot, Walter, 55
Pitt, William, 80
Poe, Edgar Allan, 67, 68, 80, 104
Pontyprid, 102
Portadown, 128

Portarlinton, 102
Portrush, 103, 106
Portsalon, 127
Portumna, 91
Price, James, 45
Puckle, George Hale, 33
Putney, 140

Radcliffe, Eddy, 50, 66, 109, 149
Rathcroghan, 21
Reilly, Paddy, 125, 126, 149
Renshaw, E., 70, 71
Renshaw, William, 71
Richardson, Canon, 38, 154
Riordan, T.J., 53
Robinson, Rev Wm. P., 34
Roscommon, 10, 18, 19, 21, 22, 29, 90, 91, 113
Roscrea, 128
Ross, Sir John, 34, 54, 155
Rosses Point, 102
Rountree, Rev James, 26, 33, 60
Rowan, Hill, 148, 157
Royle, Edward, 61

Sandringham, 14
Scotland, 52, 78, 102, 125
Shaw, Dr, 39
Shaw, George Bernard, 138
Sheelin, Lough, 51, 56
Sheldon, Helen (Lennie), 83, 87-90, 118, 119, 124, 129, 134, 135, 138, 143, 144, 145, 149, 151
Shrewsbury, 102
Skerries, 99, 106, 157
Spain, 18
Stewert, Brendan, 109
Story, Ven. Joseph, 21

St Moritz, 135
Strabane, 128
Strokestown, 10
Strokestown Park, 29, 30
Strong, L.A.G., 139
Strongbow, 2nd Earl of Pembroke, 15, 16, 17, 171
Switzerland, 134, 135, 136, 144, 151

Tennyson, 104, 151
Tongue, Alan, 7, 13, 82
Toole, J.L., 42
Toronto, 120
Tremaine, Miss Annie, 36
Trim, 17
Trinidad, 123
Trinity College, Dublin, 34, 35, 36, 41, 54
Tuam, 137
Tulsk, 10, 31
Turner, J.M.W., 151
Tynan-Hinkson, Katherine, 157
Tyrone (County Galway), 18

Victoria, Queen, 101, 103, 149

Voltaire, 151

Wales, Prince of, 36, 101, 116
Warburton, Dean & Mrs, 26, 28
Warke, 53
Warrenpoint, 106
Warwickshire, 87, 88
Washington, George, 20
Waterford, 128
Weekes, J.W., 51, 56
Wengen, 144
West Indies, 20, 117
West, L.A. Archie, 36, 38, 43
Wexford, 21, 102, 128
Whelan, Rev Mr, 53
Whitbread, Mr, 84
White, Mrs, 97
Whitton, H. Goldsmith, 80
Wilde, Oscar, 14
Windermere College, 33
Wordsworth, 151

Yeats, W.B., 14, 138, 139, 150
Youghal, 102
Ypres, 142